Cold Kitchen

A Guide to Gar de Manger

D.D. SHARMA
Head of Department
Department of Food Production
Institute of Hotel Management,
Catering and Nutrition
Pusa, New Delhi

AMAN PUBLICATIONS
NEW DELHI

Published by:
Rajiv Jain for Aman Publications
LG-4A, Ganpati Bhawan,
4675-B/21, Ansari Road,
Darya Ganj, Delhi - 110002
PH: 23255012, 23282127
E-mail: sshjbs@yahoo.com

Fist Published 2004 Reprint 2012

ISBN–81–8204–001-9

Sole Distributbor:
JINDAL BOOK SERVICES
LG-4A, Ganpati Bhawan,
4675-B/21, Ansari Road,
Darya Ganj, Delhi - 110002

Laser Typesetting by:
APCON, Delhi,
Ph: 25142551, 9811571141

Pinted by:
Tarun Offset, Delhi, India

DEDICATTION

We Dedicate this Book
to the Pious Soul of

LATE RAGHUVANSH RAJAN

Founder of
Institute of Hotel Management,
Meerut Cantt.

His immense affection and encouragement
enabled us to publish this book.
We pray that his eternal blessings
show us the path in future.

Rajiv Jain
Aman Publications

PREFACE

As a student of catering institute I always felt the need for the proper study material on cold food preparation and presentation. In our Institute there were only three copies of *Larder Chef* available in the library. The students had to wait for months to get a chance to go through this book even for a day. Mostly the books on larder were of foreign publications and hence very costly and also were not easily available. We had to depend entirely on the notes given by our teachers. Most of the students could not afford to buy these foreign publications. There was not a single Indian publication on "Larder". This was maybe because of the fact that Indians believe in freshly cooked food and there are very few cold food preparations specially cold meat preparations in India. But with advancements in travel and tourism, the Indians became interested in the art and craft of foreign cooking. Now-a-days the cold food displays in the restaurants and food exibitions have become very popular in India.

For a long time there was a need of Indian published book on Gar de Manger.

I have written this book after taking the inspiration and guidance from the *Larder Chef* written by M.J. LETO and W.K.H.D BODE and published by Heinemann, London. I have also used my observations and experience which I gathered while doing my training in gar-de-manger in the United State of America. I have also included the famous *achars, chutneys, murabbas,* and *congees* preparation from India which may be termed as our cold food items.

This books will be of a particular interest to the degree students of Hotel Management, diploma students of cookery craft, apprentices in the cook's trade and catering student in general. It will also be of value for the manager of catering establishments, especially to small hotel and restaurant owners who cannot afford specialised staff in the larder department.

I would like to thank my family members specially my son who kept encouraging and motivating me to complete this book.

D.D SHARMA

CONTENTS

1

HISTORY OF LARDER

The word 'larder' came from the word LARD meaning pork fat. Actually this name was given to the place in kitchen used as a cold storage for perishable items especially expensive ones such as meats, chicken, fish, eggs and milk etc. The French word *gar de manger* meaning "station of eatery" was an extension to cold storage that is cold food preparation and presentation, garnishing, plate and platter presentation and buffet arrangements etc. It includes the art of *charcuterie* which was very popular in ancient Romans and Greeks.

Apart from the nutritive elements derived from plants, meat from hunted wild animals was a major source of proteins and fat for ancient humans. Uncertainty of Hunter's success and enormous efforts required in the process of hunting small and big game made ancient people to domesticate some of the wild animals. Domestication could guarantee continuous supply of food. At ancient times, feed for animals were plentiful at natural pastures and in forests. As early as in the first half of the 3rd millennium BC agricultural activities and raising of domesticated animals began to develop on lands that are now the territory of Europe. From then on, developing agriculture was providing feed for domesticated animals.

Food production including supply of meat has always been determined by the level of agricultural development.

If the term of "meat processing" can be interpreted as a combination of skills required to produce food from animal meat, then we can infer that meat processing began to develop on lands that are now parts of the territory of Europe in the first half of the 3rd millennium BC. Within geographical latitudes of moderate and cold climates, ability to acquire meat was an essential factor of social development. Animals were valuable assets for the ancient people, and consumption of meat-based food was considered a cultural factor.

Prior to development of large-scale animal breeding and trade, the numbers of domesticated animals were solely dependent upon individual needs of the peasants who kept the animals. Remains of animal bones excavated from five archeological sites, located at places where ancient settlements were, indicate that before the year of 2000 BC, as well as in the early Mediaeval Ages, meat from domesticated mammals amounted to 90% of consumable meat supply. The other 10% from wild animals (deer, wild boar), and domesticated birds (hens and geese). Until 11th to 9th centuries BC people living on the territories of today's Poland consumed mainly cattle meat. Later, hogs were consumed at quantities twice as large as cattle. Mutton was seldom eaten. As regards consumption patterns, there was no difference between the inhabitants of large settlements in the Vistual River region (Vistulans tribe lands) and the smaller settlements at Western territories. Cattle were usually slaughtered at the age of 2-3 years, hogs at the age of one year or two years, sheep at the age of two years. Among the excavated bone remains there were no traces of bones of calves younger than one year.

"Natural" meat production was gradually losing its importance. It is difficult to establish when meat from domesticated animals became subject to trade transactions. Examination of bones excavated at archeological sites in

Europe as early as 2300-2000 BC. At an early stage of economic evolution it was probably a barter trade. Trade in meat, based on pecuniary valuation, began to develop not later than during the time of establishment of the first cities from 10th to 12th centuries. The first cities evolved from boroughs surrounding castles and from settlements located close to market places, they developed in result of appearance of specialized tradesmen and merchants due to growing surplus in agricultural production.

Devastation of the country during wars between local rulers and as a result of Tartar invasion prompted settlers from Western Europe. The settlers brought patterns of social organizations they were acquainted with, such as trade guilds. The first written record about the butchers, Guild in Poland, in the City of Wroclaw, comes from the year of A.D. 1175. The major facts of the history of meat industry in Poland can be found in old, written documents. The year of A.D. 1175 ends the pre-guild period of development of meat processing in Poland.

In those days cattle and hogs were raised mainly by individual peasants who kept the animals to provide fresh meat for their individual consumption, and also in order to pay tributes to the rulers. Some of the livestock was sold to the butchers and provided income to the peasants. At the same time, livestock breeding became independent from natural sources of food for animals (pastures and forests) since hay, straw and grain were more widely used as animal fodder. In close proximity to the castles and surrounding boroughs, peasants, settlements were established. Their inhabitants specialized in farming and animal breeding in order to provide food for tradesmen, craftsmen and other inhabitants of the towns.

Growing population of cities contributed to rapid increase in demand for food. The end of the 19th century brought significant changes in hog breeding. The animals were fatten in pigsties. In order to speed up maturing, domestic breeds were interbred with improved breeds such as English Yorkshire or German Edelschein.

In order to satisfy growing demand for food in cities, and to curb increasing prices, governments of all European states began to provide assistance to the farmers and supported development of livestock breeding. Commonly, examples were taken from Danish and Dutch agricultural achievements.

Butchers were one of the first skilled trade groups organized in guilds. The first written record of butchers in Europe dates back to A.D. 1175. It was then that the Count of Silesia, Boleslaw the Tall, who, upon the act of foundation, granted all income from Wroclaw butchers' stalls to the monastery in Lubiażu. The second document dates back to A.D. 1208, and relates to the transfer of title to Butchers' stalls in Trzebnica. Since the stalls could be operated only by guild members, it may be inferred that butchers' guild existed in A.D. 1175 in Wroclaw.

A document made in A.D. 1235 at Sroda Slaska relates directly to butchers guild. The number of guilds was growing in accordance with the increasing number of towns and their inhabitants.

History of development of animal slaughter houses provides evidence how development of urbanization prompted the transition of legal status of meat trade and processing. The activities lost their status as private, and became subject to public as regulations. The regulations were not only numerous but also extremely detailed. However, they were different in each town. The regulations specifically related to supplies of meat to towns, prescribed places and methods of slaughtering animals, specified places where sales of meat were allowed, and specified meat quality and prices. Examples of much detailed legal regulations relating to trade in meats date back to the time of Boleslaw the Shy (1225-1279).

At the time, butchers' guilds began building slaughter houses. The first one, managed by the guild, was established in Cracow before A.D. 1257, and then, in A.D. 1280, the second slaughter house was built by the guild in Poznan. Later, the guilds built other slaughter houses in cities. At the beginning, those were small, wooden buildings, but later, they were brick buildings. Slaughter houses were located at river banks in order to enable disposal of waste, which was simply thrown to water.

Although the slaughter houses were furnished with primitive equipment, at that time they contributed to substantial progress in improvement of sanitary conditions in cities. Livestock slaughtering was concentrated in one place, usually outside city walls, and their technical expectiveness was satisfactory. Slaughter houses also guaranteed supplies of fresh meat, inspected by skilled member of the guild. Initially, the butchers were buying livestock at the city's market place. In the 16th century purchasing animals within one mile radius from the city was prohibited. The guilds had their own pastures, and in many cases their own farms in close proximity to towns. There they kept the purchased livestock before slaughtering. Significant changes began in 19th century when municipal slaughter houses were established. Municipal slaughter houses were by far more modern, and introduction of veterinary inspection based on the then most contemporary research results, was of significant importance. Municipal slaughter houses were essential in the later development of modern meat processing.

Typical architectural structures in almost every Mediaeval City were "market" buildings, housing merchants' stalls, including butchers, stalls. Until the end of the 19th century, the stalls were the only places where sale of meat was allowed.

It can be assumed that in mediaeval ages and earlier, the price for meat was not based upon weight but was determined upon its subjective evaluation, for example, on length of sausage measured in ells. The assumption may be supported by the fact that in 1574 the butchers declared strike soon after the municipal government had ordered that price of meat should be based on weight.

Butchers' stalls were small, individual stands located in a common, wooden or brick market building. Buyers were standing outside stalls. Average floor area of a butchers' stall within the 16th century market building in Poznan was barely about 16 m^2. Early market buildings were located in town centres, i.e. in the main market place. Later, when the town grew, and the number of butchers increased, markets housing butchers' stalls were built also at other locations. Butchers' stalls were considered good investments. The guilds were purchasing the stalls from their original owners and renting them to the guild members. It is difficult to exactly establish what specific products were sold at butchers' stalls. Beyond any doubt, butchers were selling fresh meat, animal fats, semi-processed products made from marinated or smoked meats, and raw hides.

Introduction of smoked meat products including sausages is still open to research and discussions. Jewish immigrants probably brought technology of making sausages to Western Europe before or in the 14th century. It can be assumed that technology of certain processed meat products (dry sausages, raw meat semi-dry sausages, roasted sausages, liver sausages) could have been known in Europe as early as in the 13th and 14th centuries. Production of sausages and other products based on raw meat was for the first time described in Europe in the 18th century. Substantially later, technology of production steamed sausages was documented. Meat cutters were used in the process of making sausages. It has been determined that production of those sausages began in the first half of the 19th century.

In 1803 the first wieners were introduced in Vienna (Austro-Hungary). Almost century later, canned meat products were developed. Interestingly enough, first canned meat products did not attract much attention from butchers. Lack of written evidence makes it difficult to establish how butchers stored raw meat, and how did they store meat products in order to extend their "shelf life". It is difficult to imagine that only frequent slaughters and immediate sales of fresh meat prevented deterioration of quality. Similarly, it is difficult to assume that butchers were not aware of possibility of using natural ice and the method of enhancing its effectiveness by addition of salt. Butchers also stored raw meat in cellars. This assumption can be supported by the fact that there were cellars under butchers' stalls in Poznan. However, storing meat in cellars was not effective enough.

Satisfactory conditions for application of cold storage methods were developed only after establishment of new municipal slaughterhouses. Those, however, were located in bigger cities only.

Fully dependent from butchers' guilds, bazaar-like system of sale of meats was a characteristic to all of Europe. Its demise in the 19th century was also observed throughout Europe. The first butcher's stores in Paris were famous for their tasteful exterior and interior decorations, and displayed product prices in the windows. Some years later similar stores were established in Poland. In 1895, modern butcher's stores existed in Lodz. It can be considered that at the Polish territory the stores began to appear about 1880.

Development of large meat processing workshops (or manufactories) in Europe began at the same time that butcher's stores appeared. Organization of those meat-processing workshops was similar to later developed meat processing plants. The main difference between the workshops and meat processing plants was that equipment at workshops was rather primitive and the workers performed most of work. Later established meat processing plants were equipped with machines and specialized mechanical equipment to make meat products. Development of large meat processing workshops ended the guilds' exclusive rights to process meat.

Cooked meats served cold, cured and smoked and cold vegetable preparations became the mainstay of food service in Europe by 12th century.

Ancient man got introduced to meat preservation by observing the parts of carcass left on the beaches buried under the sands. The meat had become dry and flavourful because of salt. Still the curing of meats is done by salting in the similar way.

The origin of this process goes back to as far as 1500 B.C. and it is also believed that the Chinese produced same type of *charcuterie* as far back as 400 B.C. During ages a strict separation between fisheries, slaughter, butcher and prepared meat shop was enforced in order to control disease. Not until the 16th century did *charcuterie* or masters as these cooks were called legally obtain the right to butcher their own pigs and sell both raw and cooked pork products. They were permitted to sell herrings or any other salted fish during Lent, when meat products, were forbidden. As time went by fish and vegetables also showed up in their shops.

During the height of Roman Empire sausages became very popular and they enjoyed preparations from pork, chopped pine nuts and black pepper.

In 11th and 12th centuries 'Bringing home the bacon' was associated with Gifting bacon to a newly married couple for staying together for one year.

2

WEIGHTS AND MEASURES

- Dash : less than 1/8 teaspoon
- 3 teaspoons : 1 tablespoon [½ fluid ounce]
- 2 tablespoons : 1/8 cup [1 fluid ounce]
- 4 tablespoons : ¼ cup [2 fluid ounce]
- $5\frac{1}{3}$ tablespoons : 1/3 cup [2-2/3 fluid ounce]
- 8 tablespoons : ½ cup [4 fluid ounce]
- $10\frac{2}{3}$ tablespoons : 2/3 cup [5-1/3 fluid ounce]
- 12 tablespoons : ¾ cup [6 fluid ounce]
- 14 tablespoons : 7/8 cup [7 fluid ounce]
- 16 tablespoons : 1 cup
- 1 gill : ½ cup
- 1 cup : 8 fluid ounces
- 2 cups : 1 pint
- 2 pints : 1 quart [approx. 1 liter
- 4 quarts : 1 gallon
- 8 quarts : 1 peck
- 4 pecks : 1 bushel
- 1 gram : 0.035 ounces
- 1 ounce : 28.35 grams

- 16 ounces : 1 pound [435.59 grams]
- 1 kilogram : 2.21 pounds

METRIC CONVERSION TABLE

To Change	To	Multiply By
Ounces [oz]	Grams [g]	28
Pounds [lbs.]	Kilogram [km]	0.45
Teaspoon [tsp.]	Millilitres [ml]	5
Tablespoons [tbs.)	Millilitres [ml]	15
Fluid ounces [oz]	Millilitres [ml]	30
Cups [c}	Litres [lt.]	0.24
Pints [pt]	Litres [lt.]	0.47
Quarts [qt.]	Litres (lts]	0.95
Gallons [gal]	Litres [It.]	3.8
Temperature [°F]	Temp. [°C]	5/9 after subtracting 32

3

FUNCTIONS OF LARDER DEPARTMENT

In the modern-day catering business this department has become one of the most important departments, since it is dealing with expensive and mostly used food items in the business which directly affect the food cost. Chef *gar de manger* is head of this department who is assisted by the various assistant chefs and commies looking after the various aspects of cold kitchen work. The breakdown of work is generally done as follows:-

CHEF GAR DE MANGER [SR. SOUS CHEF OR SOUS CHEF]

- Chef de parties and commies, for:

(a) Butchery

(b) Charcutiere

(c) Poulterer

(d) Fish monger

(e) Chef de froid

(f) Salads and Horsdouvres (Horsdouvres)

(g) Pannier

(h) Cold storage staff

In large establishments the chef *gar de manger* will have the whole brigade but in smaller establishments he may be looking after himself with few commies. Number of staff for larder work will be depending upon the quality of cold food specialities offered by the establishment.

RESPONSIBILITIES OF CHEF GAR DE MANGER

1. He is responsible to the head or executive chef for the efficient running of his department.
2. He is responsible for the training and discipline of the Larder Staff.
3. Responsible for the storage of raw and cooked food in refrigerators, deep freezers, or other means of preservation.
4. To maintain a day-to-day record of issues made to kitchens or other departments.
5. He must study the menu in advance so as to be able to order perishables in time for the foodstuff to be prepared, cleaned, and made ready for the kitchen.
6. He must be responsible for the cleanliness, hygiene and also inform the head chef about foodstuffs, which require using.

MENU RESPONSIBILITIES ARE:

Ala Carte

- Hors d'œuvres.
- Appetizers
- Salads
- Entree

Buffet

- Cocktail receptions
- Dinners
- Conference
- Salad bars

If this department is to be run efficiently and economically, it is essential that the Chef Gar de Manger should exercise strictest possible control over the foodstuffs received and stored in the department. This involves:

- Checking the quantity and quality of all goods delivered to the larder,
- Ensuring that all foodstuffs are stored at the right temperature and that they can be easily checked;
- That the food is protected from contaimination by vermine, etc,
- That portion control is rigidly carried out e.g. a given weight of meat, or fish, or vegetables, etc., should always produce the required number of portions of steaks, fish fillets, salads, or Hors d'œuvre;
- That stock of food is regularly turned over,
- That food is not over-stocked;
- That a simple daily stock be kept by each sub-department and handed to the Chef Gar de Manger at the end of each day's business to enable him to write out his order for the following day;
- Obviously, every effort must be made to maintain the highest possible standard to hygiene, to prevent any deterioration in the foodstuffs under his control and every precaution should be taken to discourage pilfering.

Since this department is storing all the perishables required in a catering operations the chef gar de manger is responsible for ordering, quality check, storing and controlling the stocks. He has to supply such items to the various sections of the kitchen and also to the department like restaurants and bars.

To function in an effective manner, the larder department must operate in harmony with the kitchen in particular and in many cases with the pastry department, too if confusion and wastage to be avoided.

4

HORS D'ŒUVRES AND SALADS

LES HORS D'ŒUVRES

In the sequence of a modern menu the hors d'œuvres should always take the first place except on a cold winter's day when a hot soup may be preferred to a cold starter to a meal. In their present make-up hors d'œuvres were composed and developed by French chefs in the 17th century in Russia and they combined therefore originally good Russian food with French skill and finesse.

The translation of the word hors d'œuvre into any language is not easy and it is interesting how different in its meaning it is translated into other languages.

Here in India we use the words, starter, appetiser, prelude, overture, the fore-meal, the meal-before-the-meal and many other meanings are given. Side-dishe is at least in English, the most commonly used translation. This, because the original hors d'œuvres were served from the side of ball or reception room or in the anteroom before you walked into the large reception room (Side board).

Today the hors d'œuvres represent only another course in a menu and they are more often than not served on the table.

Busy restaurants serve starters from trays or trollies especially built for this purpose (big wheel effect) and in the past few years the table service has again come into the fore-front.

To be an appetiser, to make our mouths water, side dishes should at all times be colourful, appetising, piquant, varied and suitable for the time of year, occasion and meal, but most important of all they should, whenever possible, be fresh, mouth watering and attractive. To select the right dishes for the right time of year the right occasion and/or meal will not be easy.

For this reason the hors d'œuvres are placed into three basic groups with some subdivisions and this, it is hoped, will make the understanding and selection of these dishes easier.

These groups are as follows:

Group I

Single Side-dishes **Les hors d'œuvre simples**

As the heading already implies these appetisers are of one food, one portions or one dish only, with some garnish on the plate or dish.

Single hors d'œuvre can be served on plates, flats or in bowls which can be made of glass, crystal, china, eartheware, silver, wood or plastic and we call these 'plate russe'. Some side-dishes of this type may be served also in glasses, cocktail cups, beakers, e.g. cocktail crevertes roses, which are suited in presenting this type of dish.

Section A

Fruit-based side dishes

Avocado	:	with various dressings and fillings
Grapefruit	:	halves chilled, grilled, cocktails, juices
Melons	:	honeydew, cantaloup, water, charentais, ogen, cocktail
Oranges	:	cocktail, with other fruits, juice

Pineapples : cocktail, with other fruits, juice

Salads : various fruit-based compound salads

Tomatoes : stuffed with various fillings, juice

Section B

Single egg side dishes

Oeufs farcis : stuffed egg in various forms and fillings

Mayonnaise : egg mayonnaise in various presentations

d'oeufs

Salades : egg salads in various presentations

Section C

Single fish side dishes

Smoked : buckling, eel, herring, salmon, sprats, trout, roes, etc.

Fresh Pickles : soused Dieppoise, Portuguese

Bottled and Tinned : Sardines, herrings, rollmops, bismark, tunny-fish, pilchards, etc., and potted fish and shellfish

Fresh : Lobster, crab, crawfish, crayfish, oysters, mussels, cockles, etc.

Salads : There are a great number of fish and shellfish salad cocktails and mayonnaises suitable as hors d'œuvres, e.g.

Salade fecampoise fish,

Cocktail au crevettes roses prawns,

Mayonnaise de'homard lobster,

A number of compound fish and shellfish salads are also suitable.

SECTION D

Single meat side dishes

Smoked	:	various hams, turkey, venison
Charcuterie	:	various hams, raw and cooked salamis of German, Danish, Belgian, Dutch, Italian and French origin. Various liver sausages, garlic sausages, beer sausages, tongue sausage, ham sausage, mortadella and many more.
Meat	:	pies of pork, veal, ham, game, poultry preparations potted meats, brawns, realities pâtés of goose, chicken, veal and pork

GROUP II

Section of side dishes **Les hors d'œuvres variés**

Hors d'œuvres variés are served in small oblong dishes called "raviers" which can be made from crystal, glass, earthenware, china, wood or plastic and these are again placed on trays, trollies or tables for the presentation to the guest.

As the customer may choose from several or a little from all of the offered delicacies we build in a sort of portion control by cutting the items of food to be used much smaller, into various shapes like dice, strips, or paysanne to allow for a controlled service.

A soused herring which, as a single hors d'œuvres, may be given whole or as 2 fillets, in the case of a selection of starters will most likely be filleted and the fillets cut into two pieces, thus giving four smaller portions, more suitable if the guests have, shall we say, eleven other items to choose from.

The number of foods and dishes to be included in a selection of side-dishes are varied and many, and so the subsections below should help in the choice of the right items, taking into account their cost as well as the time of year and the courses to follow the hors d'œuvres.

Section A

Many of the food and dishes suitable are given in Group I above but it should be remembered that many of the single side-dishes are quite expensive, e.g. caviar, goose liver pâté, oysters and smoked salmon to name the obvious ones. It must be stressed again that in the case of hors d'œuvres varies the guest has a choice of, on average, some 12 items and the cost when making one's selection as well as this choice must be kept in mind.

Section B

Simple Salads

Beetroot, cucumber, potato, macedoine, tomato, celery, radishes, etc.

Compound Salads

Based on fruits, vegetables, meat, fish.

à la greque of	:	onions, cauliflower, celery, leeks, etc.
Portugaise of	:	onions, cauliflower, celery, mushrooms, herrings, mackerel, sprats, eel.

Section C

Tinned and	:	onions, gherkins, cucumbers, olives, etc.
bottled roots		
Pickles	:	sardines, tunny, herring, rollmops, etc.

PRESENTATION

It has already been said that side-dishes should be fresh, colourful, piquant and varied and this does apply to the hors d'œuvres varies in particular. One of the common faults, however, is that a hors d'œuvre varies is over decorated, usually with lettuce, making it appear more like a salad than a side-dish. One should realise that one has a selection of different foods, flavours and colours already, whereas a little lettuce here and there as a garnish is acceptable, it should not be over used in the presentation of a varied side-dish. One should look on the overall picture of the selection and with its different foods and colours we find a built-in colourful presentation.

One should also remember freshness and eye appeal and reduce the use of bottled and tinned food to a minimum of a quarter or third in one average. The selection of twelve foods or dishes may look like this:

Cucumber Salad (pale green)	Sweetcorn and Red Peeper (yellow, red)
Sardines in oil (silvery)	Stuffed olives (dark green/red)
Tomato salad (red)	Potato salad (white yellow)
Egg mayonnaise (yellow)	Beetroot sald (dark red)
Mushroom Portugaise (pink)	Tunny Salad, onions (light brown white)
Beef salad Provencale (grey brown)	Salami gherkin fans (red/green)

Whether single or selected side dishes, we should always be concerned with their best possible presentation. As the hors d'œuvres are usually the first dish or dishes the guest will see, we should make the best possible first impression. This can be done in many ways:

— Selecting the right dish, plate, flat, ravier for presentation

— Making sure it is clean, not chipped or cracked

— Making sure it is of the right size, not too large or too small

— Selecting the right garnishes and accompaniments

— Using the correct flat, trolley or tray on which to present

— Serving at the correct temperature (chilled).

SALAD AND HORS D' OUVERS

Mayonnaise

Mayonnaises is a semi-solid emulsion of edible vegetable oils, eggs (whole or yolks), vinegar and/or lemon juice and seasonings. Government regulations state that commercially prepared mayonnaise shall contain not less than 50% vegetable oils and the sum of oil and egg yolks shall not be less than 78%. Some products that employ starch pastes to aid emulsification and do not otherwise comply with standards for mayonnaise are commercially termed salad dressing.

Excellent commercially prepared mayonnaise may be purchased. This eliminates the general preparation of mayonnaise in the kitchen. However, some operations still make their own, and knowledge of the preparation of mayonnaise will prove valuable in emergencies.

Preparation of Mayonnaise that will stand up well and not separate involves certain factors and techniques:

Cold oil is difficult to break up into small fat globules; that affects ease of emulsification. It is recommended that oil and eggs be at room temperature for ease in obtaining emulsification.

An emulsion is more readily achieved when all ingredients are at the same temperature.

Although whole eggs are entirely suitable in the preparation of mayonnaise, egg yolks are a more efficient emulsifying agent because of their ability to hold additional fats. Fresh eggs are superior to aged or frozen eggs for use in mayonnaise. Frozen eggs, upon thawing are more liquid and a larger quantity is required than of fresh eggs. Egg yolks and salt are beaten together in the initial preparation step, prior to the addition of oil.

Rapid and thorough beating of the eggs and oils in the beginning step is one of the most important factors in producing the initial emulsion.

The method of adding oil is a deciding factor to the stability of the emulsion. **Oil must be added slowly in the beginning and in small quantities.** Once the emulsion begins to form, the oil may be added more rapidly and in greater volume, but in quantity not to exceed the volume of emulsion already formed.

The lemon or vinegar may be added at various intervals during the mixing alternately with the oil, or when a large percentage of emulsion is formed. Vinegar will thin the emulsion and make it more liquid. It also reduces the intensity of the yellow colour of the egg yolks.

Separation may occur if:

(1) oil is added too fast;

(2) oil is added in too large volume at one time;

(3) improper or inefficient mixing methods are used;

(4) ingredients are at wrong temperature.

Breaking or separating may be corrected by various methods:

(1) starting new with fresh egg yolks;

(2) starting new with a small quantity of prepared mayonnaise;

(3) the third method and the cheapest way to bring back mayonnaise which is broken, is to add the separated product to two tablespoons of warm water.

(4) Take little mustard powder, make a past with vinegar. Add broken mayonnaise slowly & keep mixing till emulsification is reformed.

It is obvious that re-emulsifying requires additional labour and time. Strict observance of prescribed methods and procedures will lessen the possibility of separation and minimize the necessity of the additional step.

Fresh mayonnaise should be stored in a refrigerator. Commercial made mayonnaise does not normally require refrigeration unless mixed with other products. A thin film of oil will form on the top of mayonnaise that has been opened and remains exposed to the air. This is not harmful and may be incorporated by simply mixing it with a spoon.

French dressing and mayonnaise provide the basis from which nearly all other dressings are made. These are the mother sauces as applied to salad preparation.

BASIC RECIPE

Raw egg yolks	5
Salt	7 g
Oil	900 g
Vinegar or lemon juice	2 tblspn
Water	2 tblspn.
Yield	1.1 lit

Method

Select an oil-repelling bowl.

Add 5 egg yolks and 7 g salt and beat it until foamy. Slowly add the oil drop-by-drop at first, then faster add the oil. When mixture becomes heavy and sticks to your whip, add 2-tablespoons of lemon juice or vinegar and the rest of the oil together with the 2 tablespoons of water.

We believe no other flavouring should be added to the basic mayonnaise as such would overpower the various flavours of sauces to be made.

NOTE: If acid/fruit juices are used, omit vinegar/ lemon juice.

For recipe calculation, each egg yolks will absorb up to 180 ml of oil.

COLD SAUCES

Cumberland Sauce **Sauce de Cumberland**

Thinly peeled orange and a little lemon peel cut into very fine julienne (strips) and blanched in boiled water. Then cooked soft in red wine, red currant jelly, one spoon of pureed Lingonberries, a little dry mustard (mixed smooth with some of red wine), season this sauce with the juice of the peeled orange and lemon, a little horseradish and a touch of cayenne pepper (serve cold).

For the orange and melon julienne, only fresh fruit should be used. If the fruit is chemically treated, the fruit should be washed well with a solution of boiled vinegar (1 part) and water (1 part).

Suggested uses: for cold game roast, game birds, pate and terrines.

Oxford Sauce **Sauce de Oxford**

Cumberland sauce without julienne of orange and lemon peels. Only grated zest of the fruit is added, season with some ginger.

Sauces derived from Mayonnaise	Flavour change derived from	Suggested Use
Mayonnaise sauce Sauce Mayonnaise	Worcestershire Sauce Prepared Mustard, Lemon Juice	Seafood, fish, eggs, meat poultry, wegs, & any kind of salad
Andalusian sauce Sauce Andalouse	Tomato paste, Julienne of red Pepper (pimento)	Eggs and meat dishes
Chantilly sauce Sauce Chantilly	Lemon Juice, Cayenne Pepper Whipped Heavy Cream	Asparagus, Artichokes, Fruit Salads
Gloucester sauce Sauce Gloucester	Dry Mustard, Chopped, Blanched Fennel, Sour Cream	Salmon, meat dishes
Green Sauce Sauce Verte	Blanched and pureed, fresh Sorrel, Spinach leaf, Watercress, Chervil, Tarragon, Parsley, Shallots:	Eggs, seafood, cold and warm fish dishes
Herb Sauce Sauce Revigote	Chopped fresh Parsley, Chervil Tarragon, Chives and Dill	Seafood, fish (cold/hot), meat dishes

Remoulade Sauce Sauce Remoulade	Chopped pickles, capers, onions, anchovies, parsley, chervil, tarragon, mustard	Fried fish and cold beef

Sauces derived from Mayonnaise	**Flavour change derived from**	**Suggested Use**
Russian Sauce Sauce Muscovite	Diced lobster and caviar	Fish and seafood
Tartar Sauce Sauce Tatare	Mayonnaise, chopped onions and relish or chopped pickles	Fried fish and cold roasts
Austrian Sauce Sauce Tyrolienne	Diced, balanced tomatoes, chilli sauce, tarragon, parsley, shallots	Seafood, fish, eggs, meat

Suggested uses: cold game roast, game birds, pate and terrines.

English Sauce **Sauce de Anglaise**

Apple sauce seasoned with grated horseradish some grated orange zest and orange juice.

Suggested uses: cold game roast, pork roast, boiled ham, turkey roast, goose and duck.

Perppermint Sauce **Sauce de Menthe**

Wine vinegar cut by half with water, add chopped, fresh mint and sugar and rest for one hour, covered.

NOTE: If dried mint is used, bring to a boil, then cool.

Suggested uses: lamb and mutton roast (hot and cold).

Criciche Sauce **Sauce Criciche**

Hard boiled egg yolks is pureed and mixed together with mustard, vinegar, salt and pepper. Then oil is whipped in until mayonnaise consistency is reached. Fold in julienne of egg white, capers, diced pickles, chopped chervil, tarragon and parsley.

Suggested uses: fish (hot and cold), boiled calves head (warm) boiled beef (cold).

Horseradish Sauce **Sauce Creme de Raifort**

Freshly grated horseradish marinated in vinegar or lemon juice folded under whipped cream. Season with sugar and salt.

Suggested uses: cooked fish (hot and cold), smoked salmon, smoked trout, boiled ham (hot and cold), boiled beef (hot and cold), hert cook eggs.

BUTTER COMPOUNDS

Fresh butter enhances through it's fine aroma the taste sensation of food products and gives it fine body.

BUTTER MIXTURE	INGREDIENTS	USAGES
WHIPPED BUTTER BEURRE BATTU	lemon, salt cayenne	fish, seafood, vegetables
TRUFFLE BUTTER BEURRE DE TRUFFES	reduction of madeira, truffles, fond & demigalce, diced truffles,cayenne salt.	sauces, fish, seafood, medallion of veal, liverwurst, canapes w/veal or chicken
CAVIAR BUTTER BEURRE DE CAVIER	Lemon juice, caviar, little whipped cream	fish, seafood
SNAIL BUTTER BEURRE POUR ESCARGOTS	shallots, garlic, parsley, lemon, worcestershire sauce, pepper, salt, pate spice	snails
SHALLOT BUTTER BEURRE D'ECHALOTTE	finely chopped shallots, little lemon juice	soups, sauces, fish, seafood, meat, vegetables, mushrooms, potatoes
BERCY BUTTER BEURRE BERCY	reduction of white wine, shallots parsley, lemon, pepper, salt, blenched beef marrow	Sauces, fish, meat, vegetable

BUTTER MIXTURE	INGREDIENTS	USAGES
COLBERT BUTTER BEURRE COLBERT PARSLEY BUTTER BEURRE MAITER D'HOTEL	parsley, glace de viande. lemon, salt, pepper. parsley, lemon, salt, pepper	Fish, seafood, meat, roasts, canapes w/eggs sauces, fish, seafood, poultry, meat, sausages roast, canapes
HERB BUTTER BEURRE RAVIGOTTE	pureed parsley, tarragon, chervil chives, watercress, shallots, lemon, salt, pepper.	soups, sauces, fish, sea- food, canapes w/cavinar, roasts, sausages
HORSERADISH BUTTER BEURRE DE RAIFORT	grated horseradish, lemon, salt	fish, meat, canapes of smoked salmon, eggs, ham, roast beef, tomato
RED WINE BUTTER BEURRE MARCHAND DE VEIN	reduction of red wine, shallots, glace de vinande, parsley, lemon, salt, pepper	sauces, fish, meat, vegetables canapes from fish and roasts
*CRAWFISH/SHRIMP BUTTER BEURRE D'ECREVISSCO	pureed boiled crawfish or shrimp shells, knife tip tomato paste, lemon, salt pepper	soups, sauces, canapes w/eggs, seafood
*LOBSTER BUTTER BEURRE DE HOMARD	boiled lobster shells, lobater eggs, lobster (coral) marrow, lemon, salt, pepper	soups, sauces, canapas w/eggs, seafood.

Cold Butter Mixture

Cold Butter Mixture are used in:

1. Finishing soups and sauces
2. As a garnish for steaks, fish, lobster and vegetables
3. To stuff snail shells
4. To cover toasts or croutons

Method: The fresh butter is set into a stainless steel bowl and kept warm until semi-soft, then whipped to a creamy consistency. Only then are the rest of the ingredients added.

NOTE: Butter should not be used melted as it loses its stability. Melted and hardened butter becomes lumpy. Only fresh ingredients give full aroma. Freshly chopped herbs should be used. Whipped creamy butter, truffles or caviar butter mixtures should not be refrigerated but used semi-soft. For butter rolls (2 centimetres) moist aluminum foil or plastic wrap should be used, then refrigerate items. Butter compound rolls should be cut into disks and according to its use, set a lettuce leaf, then lemon or sliced egg, or celery stick. This will prevent it from melting too fast.

Hot Butter Mixture

There are also hot butter compounds used in our kitchens today. These mixtures are used to enhance food and taste appeal.

SALADS

Introduction to Salads

The idea of eating uncooked vegetables for health reasons was an early one in the Mediterranean. Greek doctors and herbalists of the first and second centuries A.D. agreed that lettuce is for the stomach. There were other pleasing effects, too. Chicory "provoked venery" (no one thought it worth mentioning that its slightly bitter leaves make all the difference to lettuce salad). Lettuce (*Lactuca sativa*) was said to benefit nursing mothers because of its milky sap - hence the name Lactuca. Best of all, it soothed people to sleep.

To the Greeks and Romans, uncooked did not mean untreated. Salad derives from *sal*, meaning salt, for the green leaves were preserved in brine, then in salt and vinegar, and fresh salads were dressed with a vinaigrette dressing.

Then, as now, lettuce was the main salad ingredient. Chicory was recommended for winter time, as was endive. The name of these two plants are confusing. Curly, mop headed endive (*Cichorium endivia*) and a related variety *batavia*, with long crisp ragged leaves, are known in France and in the United States as *chicoree* and *escarole* or *batavia*. The blanched shoots of chicory (*Cichorium intybas*: to the French and Americans, endive) were first produced in their packed, yellowish-white form by the head gardener at the Brussels Botanical Garden.

Watercress, another ancient salad plant was mainly picked from books and springs until the nineteenth century when it was commercially grown.

Two essential virtues of a salad are crunch and bite. The crispness of certain lettuces of batavia and chicory can be underlined with celery and Florence fennel. Plants which add zest are sorrel, purslane and mustard and cress. These small, pointed flavour, along with herbs and a variety of oil and wine vinegar dressings, make the daily salad a gastronomic necessity.

Salads have a recognized and important place on the menu and make a nutritious and refreshing contribution to the lunch or dinner meal.

Fruits and vegetable salads are the most popular and are one of the best things of introducing valuable vitamins, essential minerals, and colour into the meal.

There are many varieties of salad greens and many are others available the year round. But the quality and price may vary according to season to season. There are other greens that are used as salad greens, such as cabbage, spinach, and watercress.

Using the Proper Amount of Dressing

Overdressing (drawning) salads is a common mistake. Salads should be only lightly coated with dressing and should never appear to be sopping wet. As a guideline, approximately three tablespoons of vinaigrette is sufficient to coat two servings of salad.

Using the Correct Procedure for Dressing a Salad

Leaf salads should always be carefully "tossed" in a sufficient large bowl with the dressing to lightly coat all of the leaves. Green should always be dressed first, then plated. It is correct to plate a salad and then pour dressing over the top. If, after tossing the greens and plating them a pool of dressing is left in the bottom of the bowl, you have used too much dressing.

Proper Plating

As with all plated food, salads should not be placed on the rim of the plate; and they certainly should never hang over the edge.

The most common mistake in plating a salad is choosing a plate that is too small. Salad greens should fit comfortably in one layer on the plate. They should be attractively arranged and, depending on plate used, either slightly rounded or flat. It is best to imagine yourself as the customer and determine whether you would be able to gracefully handle the salad greens with a fork on the plate you have chosen. Again, when in doubt, a larger plate is better than a smaller one.

SUMMARY

A properly executed green salad can be one of the most enjoyable courses in any meal. This, however, is rarely the case as the importance of the salad course, and the difficulty in preparing it, are typically underestimated.

A tossed salad appears to be very simple, but as is usually the norm, "simplicity is deceiving in that it is often the most difficult thing to achieve."

Leaf Salad Guidelines

The word "salad", as it is used today, had come to mean many things - from marinated meats, pastas or seafood to vegetables suspended in flavoured gelatin. Salad, in its original form, however, comes from the Latin phrase, "*herba salata*", which literally means "salted greens".

This variety of salad is often referred to as green, leaf or tossed salad. The primary intent is to refresh or restimulate the palate. The salad course is one of the two most frequently abused components of a meal (the other being vegetables and starches). In "professional" kitchens, salads are all too often dealt with as after thoughts or as a menial task - not worthy of anyone's real attention and effort. This being the case, the salad course becomes an ideal way to favuorably impress a customer because, again, the majority of salads that are served are poorly done.

Salads, as they are referred to today, can be broken down into four applications:

(1) served as a salad course

(2) served as an appetizer

(3) served as a main course

(4) served as an accompaniment of garnish.

These guidelines will only address salads served as a **salad course** because the majority of salads served in this country, either by home cooks or professionals, fall under this heading.

The components of a salad served as a salad course should be:

(1) fresh lettuce leaves (either a single variety or an assortment) and

(2) a light dressing (ideally a vinaigrette-type).

Although vegetables, croutons and other garnishes can, at times, be acceptable, their use should **not** become the standard. Our philosophy toward the salad course man perhaps best be summed up with this saying: "A perfect, green salad is the model of simplicity."

The most important points in the making of a green, leafy or tossed salad are:

(1) use of quality ingredients

(2) proper cleaning of the leaves

(3) proper drying of the leaves

(4) assuring that the leaves are of the proper size

(5) proper ratio of vinegar to oil

(6) using the proper amount of dressing

(7) using the correct procedure for dressing

(8) proper plating

To be more specific:

Use of Quality Ingredients

In all types of cookery, the use of quality ingredients is essential. By "quality" we do not necessarily mean "expensive." Freshness, crispness, unblemished leaves, colour and taste are all on the critical checklist for quality lettuces. If you do not start out with quality, you will not finish with quality.

Proper Cleaning of the Leaves

If excess water is allowed to remain on the lettuce, the flavours of the dressing will be diluted once they are mixed. Therefore, thorough drying is a must. The leaves can first be drained in a colander or perforated pan (do not place too much lettuce in one container, as you could bruise the leaves), then dried either by mechanical drier or by hand method (spread on sheet pans lined with absorbent towels). It may even be necessary to pat the leaves dry individually.

Assuring that the Leaves are of the Proper Size

Determining the proper size of salad greens can be hard to spell out in very specific terms. The leaves should be left in natural shapes; therefore, it is seldom that they should be cut with a knife. Pieces of lettuce should be manageable. By that we mean that a person should be able to easily get the lettuce onto his fork and into his mouth without looking or feeling clumsy. When in doubt, it is better to have larger leaves than smaller ones.

Using the Proper Ratio of Oil to Vinegar

The key point is a proper balance of acid to oil. In general, we use the basic ratio of three parts oil to one part vinegar. This formula holds true in most cases.

An example of an exception to the rule can be found in this formula:

VINAIGRETTE GOURMANDE

1 cup	fresh lemon Juice
1 cup	sherry wine vinegar
2 cups	virgin olive oil/2 cups salad oil
½ cup	or more minced chervil
½ cup	or more minced tarragon salt and freshly ground pepper

The reason this recipe works is because lemon juice is not as powerful an acid as vinegar, and virgin olive oil is strong in taste. By increasing the ratio of acid to oil in this particular case, we have found the appropriate balance.

NOTE: If emulsified dressings are used, they should be light and thin and should not interfere with eye appeal and taste.

Salad Dressings Assaisonnements pour les salades

(a) Vinaigrette and its variations

(b) Mayonnaise-based dressing and its variations

(c) Acidulated cream and its variations

(d) Scandinavian sweet sour dressing

From these basic dressings, with certain changes and additions, here are some of the best known and most used types of dressings:

(1) Vinaigrette

3 parts olive oil

1 part malt vinegar

Salt and pepper from the mill to taste

(1) Place vinegar into a china bowl

(2) Add salt and pepper and dissolve

(3) Beat in the oil gradually until it forms an emulsion

(4) Place into bottle with perforated lid

(5) Always shake bottle well before use.

(2) Lemon Dressing

As above, using ½ part of lemon juice, instead of vinegar.

(3) English Mustard Dressing

As for vinaigrette with the addition of half teaspoon of English mustard per 450 ml, reduce vinegar in proportion.

(4) French Mustard Dressing

As for Vinaigrette with the addition of half a teaspoon of French mustard per 450 ml, reduce vinegar in proportion.

(5) Fine Herbs Dressing

Vinaigrette with the addition of one tablespoon of finely chopped herbs like parsley, chieves, tarragon, chervil, etc.

(6) Marseillaise Dressing

Vinaigrette with the addition of a half clove of garlic per 450 ml finely chopped and made into a paste with salt; reduce salt in proportion.

(7) Swiss Dressing

Mix three parts of rendered fat bacon, cut into dice, with one part of heated vinegar, salt, sugar and pepper from the mill, to taste.

(8) Tomato Dressing

Add to 450 ml Vinaigrette a 112 ml of reduced fresh tomato puree.

(9) Paprika Dressing

Add to a 450 ml of Vinaigrette 60 grams of finely chopped onions and paprika to taste.

(10) Gasconne Dressing

Marseillaise dressing, with the addition of some baked garlic flavoured flutes.

(11) Anchovy Dressing

Add two to four fillets of anchovy, rubbed through a sieve, to a 450 ml litter of Vinaigrette.

(12) Place Dressing

Vinaigrette with the addition of English mustard, chill sauce and chutney.

(13) Chiffonnade Dressing

Vinaigrette with the addition of chopped hard-boiled egg, chopped parsley and fine baronies of beetroot.

(14) Roquefort Dressing

Vinaigrette with the addition of 60 grams of Roquefort cheese, rubbed through a sieve, to 450 ml of Vinaigrette.

(15) St Regis Dressing

Vinaigrette with the addition of Worcester sauce, English mustard and paprika, to taste.

(16) Cream Dressing

Mix 4 parts of fresh cream with 1 part of wine-vinegar. Salt and mill pepper, to taste.

(17) Mustard Dressing

Mix 4 parts of fresh cream with 2 parts of made mustard, English or French. Salt, sugar and mill pepper, to taste.

(18) Escoffier Dressing

Flavour mayonnaise with lemon-juice, Worcester sauce, chilli sauce, paprika and chopped chives, to taste.

(19) Special Dressing

Flavour mayonnaise chopped tarragon, tarragon-vinegar, chopped chives; add beaten fresh cream.

Selection of Green Salads	Suitable Dressings	Les Salades Verts
Lettuce Salad	1 2 3 4 5 6 10 23 24	Salade de Laitue
Cos Lettuce Salad	1 2 3 4 5 6 10 14 15 23 24	Salade de Romaine
Endive Salad	1 2 3 4 5 6 7 10 14 15 23 24	Salade de Chicoree frisee
Chicory Salad	1 2 3 4 5 6 7 10 17 22	Salade d'Endives Belge
Watercress Salad	1 2 3	Salade Cresson des Fountain
Mustard and Cress Salad	1 2 3	Salade des Cressonnette
Lambs Lettuce Salad	1 2 3 4 5 6 7 8 9 10 23 24	Salade de Mache
Batavian	1 2 3 4 5 6 7 8 18 19 21	Salade d' Escarole
Dandelion Salad	1 2 3 4 5 6 9 14 16 21 23 24	Salade de Pissenlit
Sorrel Salad	1 2 3 4 5 6 9 10 11	Salade d'Oseille

(20) Thousand Island Dressing

Add to 450 ml of mayonnaise, 60 grams of fine diced red and green peppers; flavour with paprika and chill sauce.

(21) Chatelaine Dressing

Mix equal amounts of fresh cream and mayonnaise.

(22) Russian Dressing

Add to 450 ml mayonnaise, the following additions; 1 teaspoon finely chopped beetroot, 1 teaspoon finely diced red and green peppers, teaspoon finely chopped parsley and chieves, 1 teaspoon caviar.

(23) Dill Dressing

Add to 450 ml of mayonnaise 120 grams of chopped dill, 230 ml of single cream, an some lemon juice, salt and pepper.

(24) Scandinavian Dressing

Mix 3 parts of castor sugar with 2 parts of wine or white vinegar dissolve overnight, use with all green salads, various herbs can be added.

PREPARATION OF MOST GREEN SALADS

(1) Always wash in cold water. Hold by roots, plunging into water to force water to centre, thus removing dirt and grit. Repeat process several times, each time in clean water.

(2) Remove bad or discoloured parts. Trim roots are carefully inspect inside for slugs and insects. Remove coarse ribs from outer leaves with fingers. Place into iced water to get crisp.

(3) Drain thoroughly. Shake well in a salad basket of colander. Place on clean cloth; avoid bruising leaves. Keep in a cool place until required.

(4) Serve neatly in china, glass or wooden bowls. Garnish as required. Serve dressing apart. Always keep cool.

NOTE: Do not: wash salads under tap; allow salads to soak in luke-warm water; forget to inspect centre for slugs and insects; drain on dirty table or trays or bruise leaves; cut salads with steel knife (use fingers or stainless steel knife).

Mixed Green Salad **Salades Vertes Panachees**

It is not always realised that one can serve a mixed of green salads only e.g. some cos-lettuce, a little suitably cut chicory and some cress or mustard and cress will make an appetising display and would be most suitable for a light lunch, or as an accompaniment to all types of roast meat at Dinner or Banquet.

Dressed Green Salads

There are also to be found some dressed green salads, usually composed of one of the above green salads plus some additions or garnishes which give it a new name, they cannot be called mixed salads for only one addition for example.

Mimosa Salad **Salade Verte Mimosa**

Cos lettuce, with the addition of finely chopped or sieved yolk of egg sprinkled on the top.

Orange Salad **Salade Verte a l'orange**

Lettuce with the addition of orange segments and blanched orange peel in Julienne sprinkled on the top.

Tarragon Salad **Salade Estragon**

Lettuce with the addition of freshly chopped Tarragon leaves sprinkled on the top.

Special Note

The green salads are often grouped with the simple salads, but as they have quite different uses and for easy

SUITABLE DRESSINGS

Salad								French name
Artichoke Salad	1	2	12	16				*Salade d'artichaunts*
Asparagus Salad	1	2	20	23				*Salade d'asperges*
Beetroot Salad	1	2	3	4	5	6		*Salade de betterave*
Cabbage Salad red	1	4	7					*Salade de choux rouges*
Cabbage Salad white	1	4	7					*Salade de choux*
Celery Salad	1	4	7	16				*Salade de celeri*
Celeriac Salad raw	1	4	7	16				*Salade de celeri-raue cur*
Celeriac Salad cooked	1	4	7	16				*Salade de celeri-raue cuit*
Cole Slaw	1	7	17	18				—
Cucumber Salad	1	4	16					*Salade de concombre*
French Bean Salad	1	4						*Salade de haricots verts*
Haricot Bean Salad	1	4	10					*Salade de haricots blancs*
Potato Salad	1	4	5	7	10	1	8	*Salade de pommes de terre*
Radish Salad	1	4	16					*Salade de radis*
Sweetcorn Salad	1	4	5	12	18	19		*Salade de mais*
Sweet Pepper Salad	1	4	5					*Salade de piments*
Tomato Salad	1	4	5	22				*Salade de tomatoes*

recognition they are given here separately.

Simple Vegetables Salads Salades de Legumes Simple

The simple – sometimes also called plain salads – are produced from fruit or root vegetables rather than from leaves, as is the case of the green salads.

Given below are some of the simple salads prepared and eaten raw:

Cucumber, cabbage, radish, tomato etc.

Others will have to be cooked before eating, as as follows:

Asparagus, beetroot, celeriac, potato etc.

A few lend themselves for service both raw and cooked, are given below:

Cabbage, celery, Celeriac etc.

Preparation for Simple Salads

The preparation of simple salads varies from one salad to salad. No general rule can therefore be given except to use only the freshest of vegetables and much care in their dressing and presentation.

Mixed Salads Salades panachees

For a mixed salad use any of the green of simple salad, according to availability or time. Some mixed salads, however, have especially laid down rule as to their contents, some of which are given below:

French Salad Salade Francaise

The selection of salads, consisting of lettuce, tomato, cucumber, spring onions, water-cress or mustard and cress, as well as quarters of hard boiled eggs, neatly arranged into a colourful display.

Lord Salad Salade des Lords

Lettuce garnished with orange segents blanched Julienne of zest of oranges, walnuts, almonds and chives.

Salad Muguette **Salade Muguette**

Curly endives, russet apples, Julienne of Celery, tomatoes, radishes, tarragon.

Miarni Salad **Salade Miarni**

Lettuce hearts, segments of tangerines and lemons, quarters of tomatoes.

Compound Salads **Salades Composees**

The third group of salads is made from a combination of ingredients such as vegetables, fruit, fish, meats, poultry and game. They are marinaded and bound again with vinaigrette or one of its variations, acidulated cream, or one of its variations, or mayonnaise, or one of its variations.

Many of these salads are of American origin, and are often referred to as American salads, others come from all over the world. In Great Britain these types of salads are too much in used, and only a few such as Waldorf Salads are really well-known. On the Continent and in America they are very popular and found in daily use amongst all types of catering establishments.

Preparation of Compound Salads

The preparation of Compound Salads as well as the ingredients used, varies considerably from one salad to another. Again, only the best materials should be used, well washed, clean and dry.

Most salads of the compound type are bound with mayonnaise or mayonnaise collee, a mayonnaise to which aspic has been added so that the salad will set. Other salads are bound or seasoned with acidulated cream or vinaigrette or one of their variations.

Service of Compound Salads

To say where and when compound salads should be served is not at all easy because their number is great, and ingredients varied and contrasting. However, the four good uses for this type of salad are as follows:

Side Salad

Some compound salads find their first and obvious use as side salads, either with roast or some suitable fish dishes. They could also be considered for replacing at least in the summer months any accompanying vegetable normally served with dishes other than roasts or fish.

Selections of Side Dishes — Hors d'œuvre varies

Many, especially those of fruit or vegetable based compound salads, are very good to compliment and widen the range of a selection of side dishes. As could indeed some of the meat and fish based compound salads. The latter, however, can be quite expensive to produce and for this reason, cannot always be included in our selection of side dishes.

Single Side dishes — Hors d'œuvre singuliers

Those compound salads of a more substantial composition, including such items as poultry, game, meats or fish and shell-fish are ideally suited as a single appetiser.

It is pleasing to see that of late they have become more and more popular.

Cold Buffet — Buffet froid

All types of salads whether green, simple, mixed or compound, should be found on any cold buffet, however simple or elaborate its presentation might be.

Whereas green and simple salads as well as some of the fruit and vegetable based compound salads should be considered the natural accompaniment of coked meats and fish.

The more substantial of the compound salads should be considered dishes in there own right on a cold buffet Suitably garnished and well presented the colourful and piquant salads man be considered as a main dish, like a rib of beef or leg of ham. They greatly enhance and widen the contents and range of our buffet dishes.

To help to find the best use for the many compound salads, they have been grouped into four groups as to their basic composition. The four basic types are:

(1) Compound Salads with a fruit base

(2) Compound Salads with a vegetable base

(3) Compound Salads with a meat, poulty or game base

(4) Compound Salads with a fish or shellfish base.

The following list does not attempt to give all Compound Salads but only a sample of each type most commonly known and used, leaving out those which are very similar to others.

Examples of fruit based compound salads

Alice Salad	*Salade Alice*
Apple Salad	*Salade de pommes*
Creole Salad	*Salade creole*
Columbia Salad	*Salade Columbia*
Eve Salad	*Salade Eve*
Femina Salad	*Salade Femina*
Florida Salad	*Salade Florida*
Japanaise Salad	*Salade Japonaise*
Javanaise Salad	*Salade Javanaise*
Mimosa Salad	*Salade Mimosa*
Montmorency Salad	*Salade Montmorency*
Orleans Salad	*Salade d'Orleans*
Waldorf Salad	*Salade Waldorf etc.*

Examples of Vegetable-based Compound Salads

Aida Salad	*Salade Aida*
American Salad	*Salade Americane*
Andalousian Salad	*Salade Andalouse*
Bagatelle Salad	*Salade Bagatelle*
Canaille Salad	*Salade Canaille*
Watercress Salad	*Salade Cressonniere*
Italian Salad	*Salade Italienne*
Macaroni Tomato Salad	*Salade de macaroni aux tomates*
Macaroni Beetroot Salad	*Salade de macaroni aux bettraves*
Mercedes Salad	*Salade Mercedes*
Oriental Salad	*Salade Orientale*
Rice Salad	*Salade de riz*
Spanish rice Salad	*Salade de riz Espagnole*
Spanish Salad	*Salade Espagnole*
St Jean Salad	*Salade Saint Jean*
Yam Yam Salad	*Yam Yam Salad* etc.

Examples for Fish based Compound Salads

Dutch Salad	*Salade Hollandaise*
Beauty of the Night Salad	*Salade Belle de nuit*
Favoutite Salad	*Salade Favorite*
Francillon Salad	*Salade Francillon*
German Salad	*Salade Allemande*
Mignon Salad	*Salade Mignon*
Monte Cristo Salad	*Salade Monte Cristo*
Moscow Salad	*Salade Moscovite*

Paris Salad	*Salade des Parisienne*
Russian Salad	*Salade de Russe*
Scotch Salad	*Salade Esossaise*
Victoria Salad	*Salade Victoria.*

Example of Meat based Compound Salads	
Bagration Salad	*Salade Bagration*
Beatrice Salad	*Salade Beatrice*
Carmen Salad	*Salade Carmen*
Egyptian Salad	*Salade Egyptienne*
Fanchette Salad	*Salade Fanchette*
Hungarian Salad	*Salade Hongroise*
Mascot Salad	*Salade Mascotte*
Mexican Salad	*Salade Mexicaine*
Nun Salad	*Salade des Nommes*
Opera Salad	*Salade Opera*
Regency Salad	*Salade Regence*
Tosca Salad	*Salade Tosca* etc.

Garnishes and borders for compound salads

One, or several, of the following items may be used:

(1) Neat, blanched rings of onion.

(2) Slices, quarters as well as coarsely chopped eggs.

(3) Slices of beetroot, cut into diamonds, triangles, or half moon shaped

(4) Slices of truffles, cut into diamonds, triangles or half moon shaped

(5) Julienne of truffles, whites of eggs, pimentos, mushrooms, ham, tongue.

(6) Quarters or hearts of lettuce, whole or sliced radishes, cucumber, tomatoes, spring onions.

(7) Bouquets of fresh watercress, mustard and cress or asparagus.

(8) Dice, Julienne, diamonds, triangles, etc. Of the main ingredient of the salad.

(9) Base, surround or borders man also be made of crisp lettuce leaves or quartered hearts, cos lettuce or chicory.

(10) On occasin Tartelettes Barquettes as well as croutes and fleurons are very helpful in the presentation of compound salads.

Service

All salads, Simple or Compound, are best served in individual or larger crystal, glass, China or wooden bowls, called saladiers. Whereas the Green and Simple Salads can be served in the deeper saladiers, the Compound Salads whenever possible should be served on the flatter type of saladier, which will allow more room for border and garnishes which often surround this type of salad.

Some of the more expensive types of Compound Salads can be served on crushed ice. Folded or artistically shaped serviettes complete the picture.

Special Notes

A We serve a few numbers of fish, poultry, beef and some continental sausage salads, invariably they are served as single side-dishes, very occasionally served as a main course dish.

B We serve quite a number of plated salads in the more popular types of catering establishments

e.g. Ham Salad

Veal and Ham pie Salad

Egg Salad

Cheese Salad etc.

These dishes should not really be considered salads as such, but cold dishes to which salad has been added to make it a meal.

HORS D' OEUVERES AND SALADS

Recipes of Salads

Single salads — **Salade de legumes simples**

1. Tomato Salad — **Salade de tomato**

Base	¼ lettuce leaves
Body	250 g washed tomatoes, remove eyes, blanch peel and slice thinly
Dressing	50 ml vinaigrette
Garnish	10 g finely chopped parsley,

2. Russian cucumber salad — **Salade de concombres a la russe**

Base	Shredded romaine
Body	1 medium size cucumber evenly sliced
Dressing	50 ml vinaigrette with our cream
Garnish	30 g finely chopped parsley.

3. Cabbage salad — **Salade de choux cuits**

Base	¼ lettuce leaves
Body	Destalked shredded cabbage leaves 400 g, blanched in water
Drerring	50 ml acidulated cream
Garnish	30 g tomato concasse.

4. Asparagus salad — **Salade d,asperges**

Base	¼ lettuce leaves
Body	8 pieces of cooked asparagus

Dressing 50 ml lemon dressing

Garnish ½ tsp. Finely chopped parsley.

Method

Marinade asparagus for a while in lemon dressing. Add chopped herbs. Dress in a ravier on lettuce leaves with points upper most.

Compound salads **Salades composes**

5. Marinated Greek Salad with tofu **Salade de grecque**

Base Chicory

Body Tomatoes, peeled, seeded, diced, red peppers, ¼ "dice, blanched green peppers, cucumbers, peeled, seeded, ¼ "dice red onions, chopped

Dressing French dressing using olive oil and wine vinegar 2: 1, oregano, cubed tofu marinated in dressing, green olive

6. Tortellini salad **Salade Italinne**

Base Chicory

Body Tortellini or any pasta, pesto, salami, red onions, celery, red peppers, green peppers, tomatoes, peeled, seeded and diced

Dressing Italian dressing [vinegar, olive oil, seasoning, basil, oregano, minced onions, garlic]

7. Kokonda spicy **Salade de Poisson a l'Africaine**

1. African salad

Base Boston lettuce

Body White fish, cooked, flaked, lemon juice, red peppers seed bananas sliced, green peppers, seeded, shredded, fresh coconut, grated, tomatoes, peeled, seeded, diced, pineapple Chunks.

Dressing Sour cream with minced green chillies, ground cumin seeds, Seasoning.

8. Wurstalat **German salad**

Base Iceberg shredded

Booby Cooked German sausages, skinned and sliced, green peppers sliced thin, red peppers sliced thin, onions sliced thin

Dressing Salad oil, cider vinegar, dry mustard, paprika, seasoning, crushed.

Garnish Gherkins.

9. Mexican corn salad **Salade de mexicaine**

Base Chicory

Body Whole corn [frozen, canned or fresh], green peppers diced, green chilies chopped, Mexian green tomatoes diced, red onions, zucchini small diced, mild cheese tomatoes peeled, seeded and diced

Dressing Olive oil, salad oil, fresh lemon juice, oregano, ground cumin, seasoning

Garnish Black olive with parsley

Dressing Olive oil, salad oil, fresh lemon juice, oregano, ground cumin, seasoning

Garnish Black olive with parsley

Method

Marinate everything except tomatoes and cheese 1-2 hr. Drain and add tomatoes and cheese.

5

FISH MONGERY

Long ago fish was eaten only on seasides and eventually along rivers and ponds. Today with progress of transport and refrigeration fish can be found and eaten all over the world.

Fish is probably the world largest reserve and source of proteins. Even if some oceans are fished extensively, nature, renews the stock and will keep on doing so if pollution does not get worse. In the EEC, fish catch is limited so that the markets are not flooded with products and that ecology of the sea is respected.

In India peoples habit tends to place white pomfert at the top but there are many more at least as good as this one. Fish is fragile, as it does not contain many connective tissues, its flesh does not keep as well as meat and care must be taken in choosing and storing it.

CLASSIFICATION

Fish can be divided in two main families,

(A) Finfish.

(B) Shellfish or sea food [Fruits de Mer]

Finfish can be divided into flat fish and round fish.

Real flat fish has its two eyes on the same side. Round fish has one eye on each side. Pomfret has one eye on each side but its shape is more of a flat than a round fish.

Shellfish or seafood is sub-divided into three types:

(A) Crustaceans: They have 8 legs. A head and a tail [except crab]. No internal skeleton.

(B) Molluscs: They have one shell or a double shell. No internal skeleton.

(C) Ceplacopodes: Squids, calamar, octopus. Head between the body and 8 tentacles.

Coming back to finfish, we see that there fat content vary from species to species.

Lean fish 0.5% to 5%

Fat fish 5% to 20%

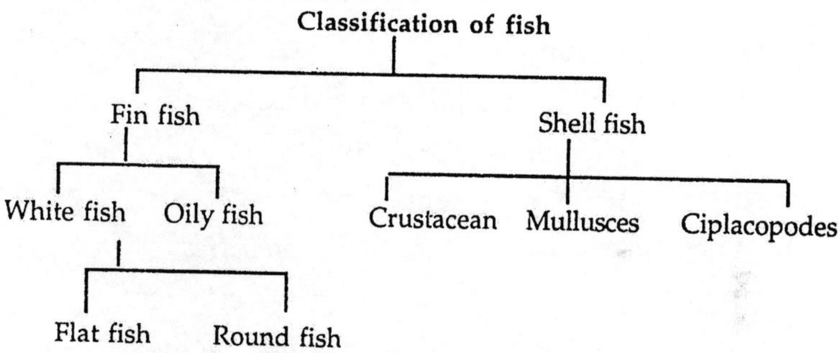

White fish (demersal)

Round		Flat	
English	**French**	**English**	**French**
The Cod	*Le cabillaud*	The Halibut	*Le Fletan*
The Haddock	*L' Aiglefin*	Dab	*Le Carrelet*
The Whiting	*Le Merlan*	The Plaice	*La Plie*
Coal fish	*Le Colin*	Sole [Lemon]	*La Limande*
Hake	La Merluche	The Turbot	*Le Turbot*
The Ling	La Lingue	The Brill	*La Barbue*
		Dover Sòle	*La Sole*

Oily Fish (Pelagic)

English	French
River Trout	*La Truite de Riviere*
Salmon	*Le Saumon*
Pike	*Le Brochette*
The Herring	Le Hereng
The Sprat	*Le Sprat*
Whitebait	*Les Blanchailles*
The Anchovy	*L' Anchois*
Mackerel	*Le Maquereal*

Some Indian Fish

Oily fish: Hilsa, Beckti and Salmon

White fish [round]—Rohu, Singara and *Surmai*

Shell fish - Crustacean

SHRIMPS	*les crevettes*
PRAWNS	*les crevette roses*
KING PRAWNS	*les langoustines*
CRAY FISH	*les ecrevisses*
LOBSTERS	*les homards*
CRAWFISH	*les langoustes*
CRAB	*les crabes*

Molluscs

OYSTERS	*les huitres*
MUSSELS	*les moules*
SCALLOPS	*les coquilles st jacques*
COCKLES	*les clovisses*
SNAILS	*les escargots*
CLAMS	*les palourdes*
WINKLES	*les bigorneaux*

Ceplacopodes

Squids

Calamar

Octopus.

Quality checklist for fish. It is done on 5 points:

	Fresh	Not fresh
1. Smell	mild	fishy strong
2. Eyes	protruding	sunken
3. Gills	red	brown grey
4. Flesh	elastic	soft
5. Body	firm	flabby

Scale is not a good criterion as some fish loose their scale if fresh, other keep them even if not fresh.

Storage of Fish

The objective of storing fish is

— to keep it around 0°C

— to prevent from drying

— To prevent from communicating flavour to other foods.

The best method is on crushed ice. Beware of ice burn. Wrap fillets whole fish by its own skin.

Shelf life - 2days

Frozen fish:

If you buy frozen fish check that:

— it is not thawed

— it has a fresh smell or no smell

— It has no freezer burn.

Seafoods especially molluses, should be purchased alive.

Dressing a fish:

Fish must be eviscerated as early as possible. If you do not want to use it immediately eviscerate and store.

Remove scales before evisceration because they are easy to remove.

1. **Scales:** use a fork for a small fish. A rigid knife for a large fish. Start from tail to head. Work in a sink [scales will not fly]. Remove scales in the bin and then rinse sink and fish. Check that no scales are left.
2. **Gutting:** Large fish are open from anal fin to gills. Small fish from gills only [not to damage its shape]. Remove viscera and gills, save ROE and eggs.
3. **Fins:** Cut all fins with knife and pare tail. If serving whole do not cut head otherwise remove it.

CUTS OF FISH

1. **Fillet:** cut without bone
2. **Darne:** 1 cm thick slice of a round fish on the bone.
3. **Tronçon:** 1 cm thick slice of a flat fish on the bone.
4. **Supreme:** boneless side of fish.
5. **Delice**: a folded fillet of fish.
6. **Paupiette**: a rolled fillet of fish.
7. **Goujon:** fillet of fish cut in to finger size pieces.

To Fillet a Flat Fish

(1) Make an incision down the centre of the backbone from head to tail with the fish flat on the board

(2) With the tips of fingers of the left hand, feel along the bones and roll the flesh away from the ridge of the backbone.

(3) Next separate the top of the left fillet, near the

head, with the tip of the filleting knife.

(4) Now, with the blade of the knife flat on the bone of the fish, cut outwards towards the fins, from head to tail.

(5) At the same time, roll the fillet to the left of the bones with the fingers of the left hand, so as to follow the bones closely, and remove the fillet without damage the flesh.

(6) Now turn the fish round, so that the head of the fish is nearest to the body and repeat the operation, this time cutting outwards from tail to head.

(7) Turn the fish over and repeat on the reverse side.

(8) Next, skin the fillets, trim the edges, wash dry with a clean cloth and place on a clean tray.

To Fillet a Round Fish

(1) Place the fish on its side on the board, after cleaning, naturally.

(2) Make an incision along the bone—close to one side of the dorsal fins, about 1 cm in depth from head to tail.

(3) Run the fingers of the left hand along the cut to feel the bones and separate the flesh from them by pushing the flesh to the left of the backbone.

(4) Now, with the tip of the knife, scrape over the ribs of the flesh from head to tail, folding the flesh back with fingers of the left hand, so as to follow the bones without cutting in to flesh.

(5) When near the tail, insert the blade of the knife between the fillet and the bones, by placing the fillet over it.

(6) Cut off the fillet neatly, by drawing the knife-edge from head to tail.

(7) Skin the fillet, pull out any bones you can feel with your fingers, trim, wash, dry and place on a clean tray.

Some important preparation for fish cooking

Fish Marinade

1/8 litre oil

1/8 white wine

2 bay leaves

1 spring parsley

Juice of ½ lemon

Pinch of salt

Pinch of white pepper

Mix all ingredients, pour over fish to marinade for 30 to 60 minutes before cooking.

French Frying Batter

(1) Yeast Batter

250 gam flour

¼ litre milk or water

15 g yeast

Pinch of salt

(1) Sift flour, place in a basin with salt.

(2) Dissolve the yeast in liquid.

(3) Gradually add to flour, mixing into a smooth paste.

(4) Leave in warm place for at least one hour before use.

Quick French Frying Batter

150 g flour

¼liter milk of water

1 yolk of egg

2 whites of egg

1 tsp of oil

Pinch of salt

(1) Mix sifted flour and liquid to a smooth paste.

(2) Add egg yolk, oil and salt, mix well.

(3) Beat the two egg whites until mixture is very stiff.

(4) Gently fold into the other mixture.

(5) The batter can be used immediately.

Beer Batter

250 gm flour

¼ litre Light ale or lager

1 egg

Pinch of salt

(1) Mix sifted flour and salt.

(2) Gradually mix to a smooth paste.

(3) Add whole egg, mix well in.

(4) Leave in a warm place for about 30 to 60 minutes before use.

6

POULTRY AND GAME

The term 'poultry' is applied to all types of domesticated fowl, whether bred for the table or for its eggs. These include chicken, goose, duck, turkey and guines fowl. Poultry has become very popular because of modern farming methods and the modern trend towards healthier eating habbits with people turning away from the more traditional red meats. On the whole the poultry have a lesser fat content than other meats and are therefore easy to digest. All poultry is extremely versatile, none more so than chicken.

When choosing your bird, be careful as its needs to be very fresh. The flesh should be firm with a fine texture, and there should not be too much fat, even on ducks. The skin should be white to pale yellow and dry. The breastbone should be straight and the breasts broad and bones pink and bright. A bird that is too fresh will quickly show tinges of green around the back bone the neck and vent. The breastbone on all young birds will be pliable at the tip.

There are basically two types of game available: Feathered game and Furred game. In the first variety we have got Grouse, Partridge, Pheasant, Quail, Snipe, Wild duck, Woodcock and Wood pigeon. While in the second variety we have Hare, Rabbit, Venison and Wild Boar.

CHICKEN

Chicken is the term used to describe domesticated barnyard fowl and includes everything from baby chicken to boiling fowl.

Types of Chicken

English	French	Average weight	Average age
Poussin	Le Poussin	250 to 300 g	4 to 6 weeks
Young chicken	Le poulet de grain	350 to 600 g	6 to 8 weeks
Broiler chicken	Le poulet	800 g to 1 kg	4 to 6 months
Boiling chicken	La poule	1 to 3 Kg	12 months
Capon	Le chapon	2 to 4 Kg	5 to 8 months

Preparation, Dressing and Cuts

The birds are generally killed by cutting the neck. Larger birds are commonly stunned electrically prior to killing. The muscles or flesh of poultry will stiffen and toughen as soon as rigor mortis sets in 3 to 4 hours after killing. To avoid this the bird should be hanged for maximum 24 hours also it will help in tenderizing the bird.

Cut for Grilling **En Spatchcock**

After singing, drawing and trimming split the bird down the back along the backbone with a large knife through the body with the bird on its back on a chopping board from neck to parson nose. Flatten well with a cutlet bat, remove ribs, and trim the backbone and place neatly on a clean tray.

Cut for Sauté

Singe, wipe and draw the bird. Trim the wings, tail, knuckles and neck. Remove the wishbone. Remove the legs by cutting through the ball and socket joints. Remove the leg bone from the legs. Remove the breast pieces by cutting from the breastbone along the ribe cage on both the sides. Bring the meat of the wing bone downwards and trim the wing bone.

PLUCKING AND SINGEING

6.1. *Hold the bird in one hand. breast up and head away.*

6.2. *Using your free hand, grasp a few feathers and giving a sharp tug towards the head pull out the feathers, being careful not to damage the skin in the process.*

6.3. *Work your way back along the breasts, then the legs. Remove all the feathers in this way. The tail and wing feathers are tougher than the others and have to be removed one at a time.*

6.4. *Singe the plucked bird by passing it over an open flame, to remove the covering of fine hairs that remain.*

DRAWING

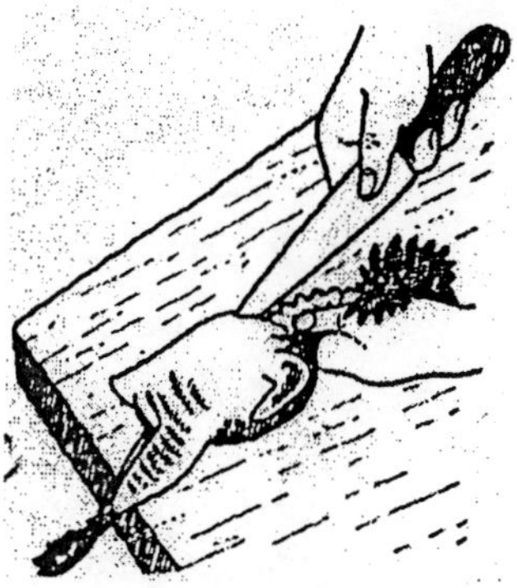

6.5. *Lay the bird on its breasts, pinch the flesh under the neck and make an incision from the base of the neck to two-thirds of the way towards the head.*

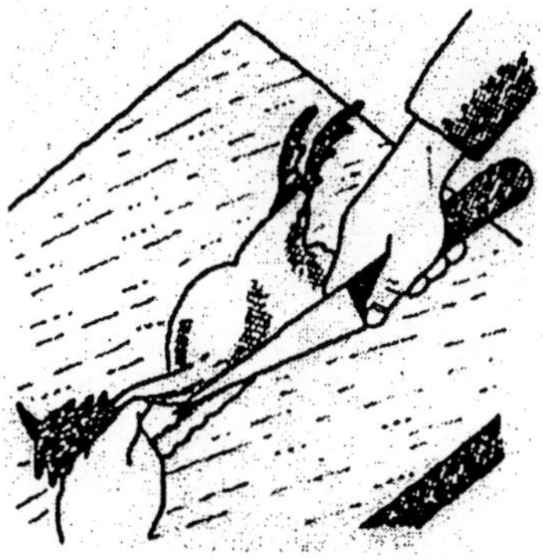

6.6. *Turn the bird on to its back. insert the point of the knife above the neck bone at its base and cu t through. Cut off the head.*

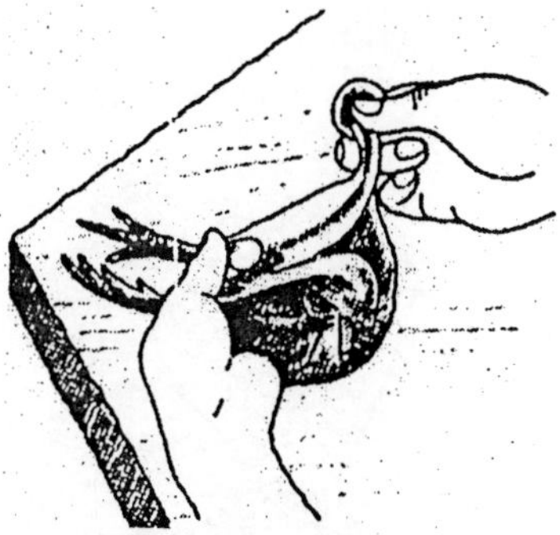

6.7. *Pull the crop away from the skin around the neck.*

6.8. *Insert your fore and middle fingers and ease the lungs away from the back bone, and free the windpipe and gullet.*

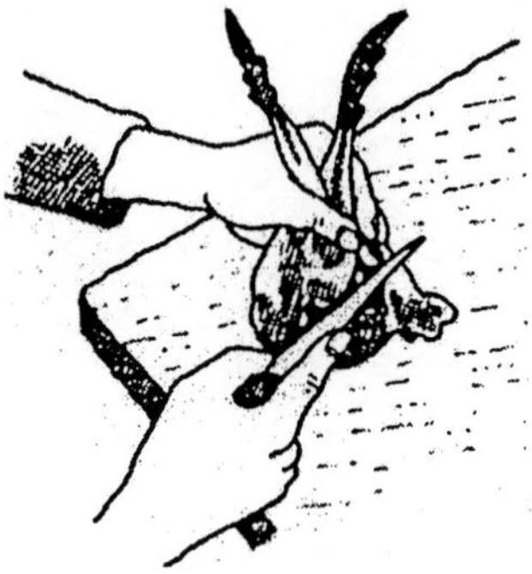

6.9 *Make a slit above the vent.*

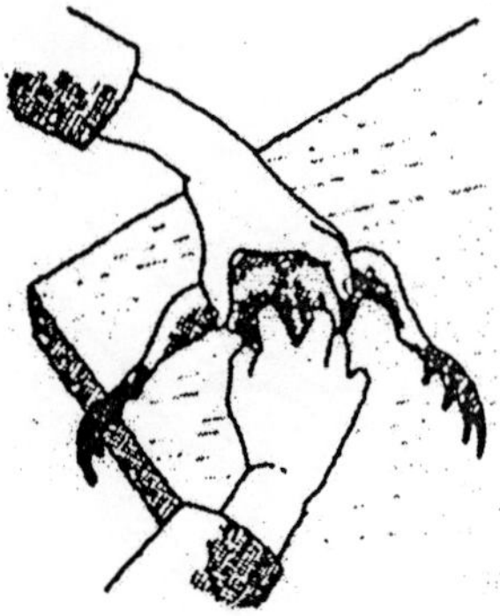

6.10. *Insert your fore and middle fingers into the slit, hook them around the stomach and pull out the entrails. Cut around the vent to remove.*

Preparing Poultry and Game

PREPARING SUPREMES

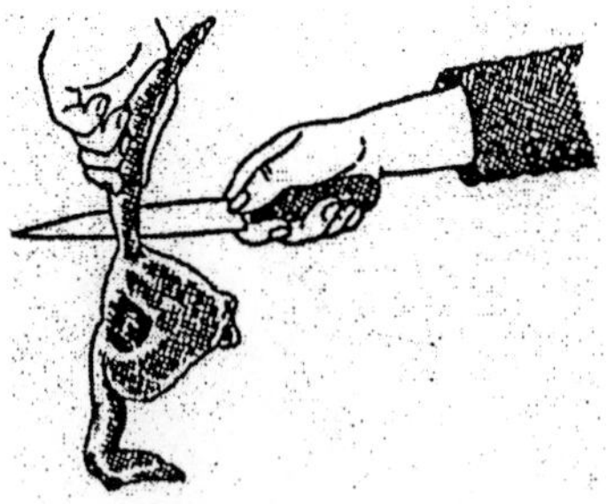

6.11. *Hold the bird aloft by one wing. Using a sharp knife, cut around the base of the wing as close to the breast as is possible. Repeat on the other wing.*

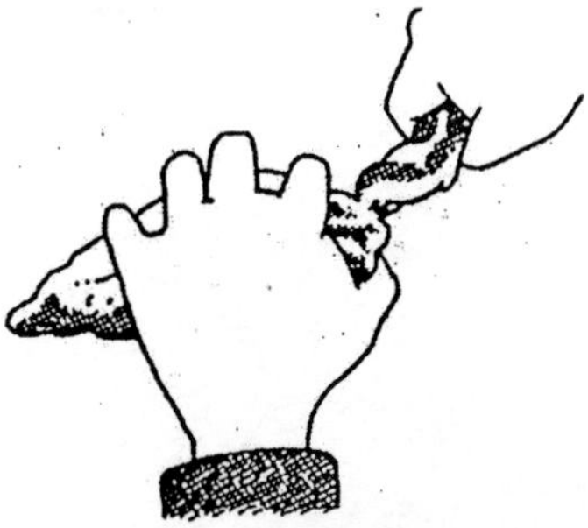

6.12. *Holding the bird steady with one hand, twist the wing against the joint and pull it off.*

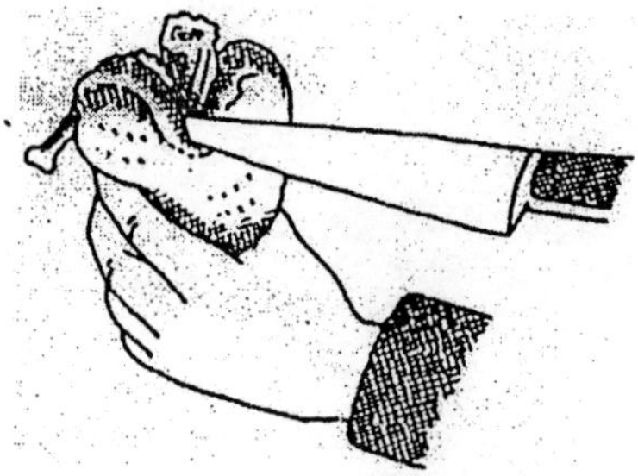

6.13. *Insert the point of the knife into the neck of the bird piroting the point on the neck bone. Twist the knife on its point, scraping it against the wish bone on both sides.*

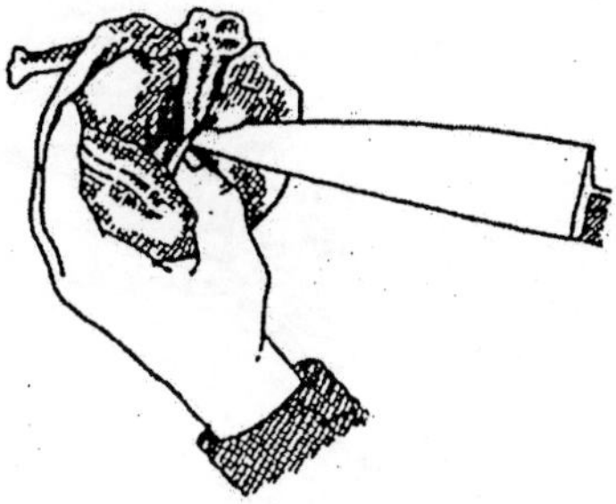

6.14. *Separate the wish bone from the flesh with your fingers and cut off the bone at the base, then pull it out.*

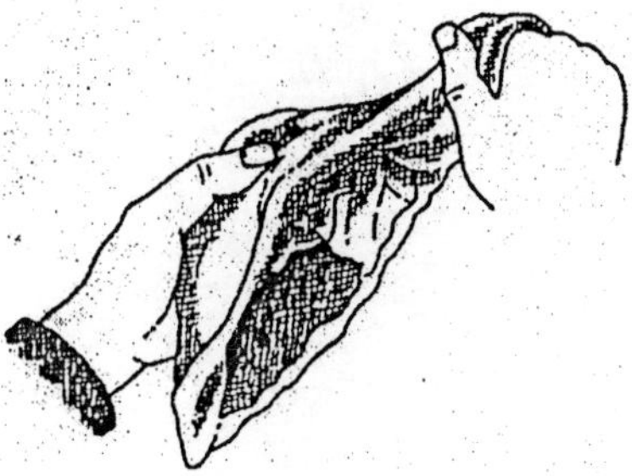

6.15. *Pull the skin away from the breasts and back.*

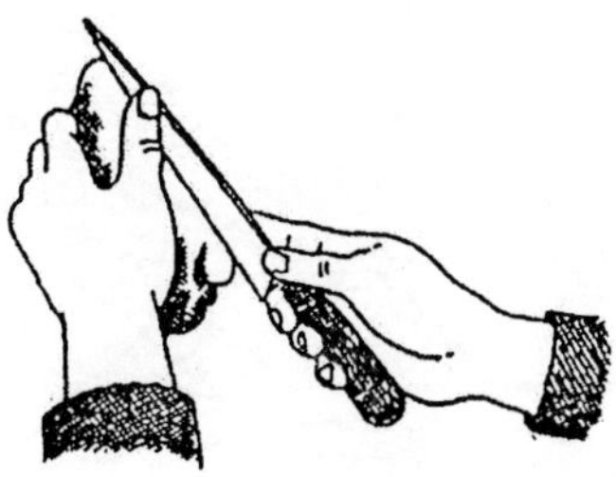

6.16. *Holding the bird in your left hand and, using a sharp knife, cut down one side of the breast bone.*

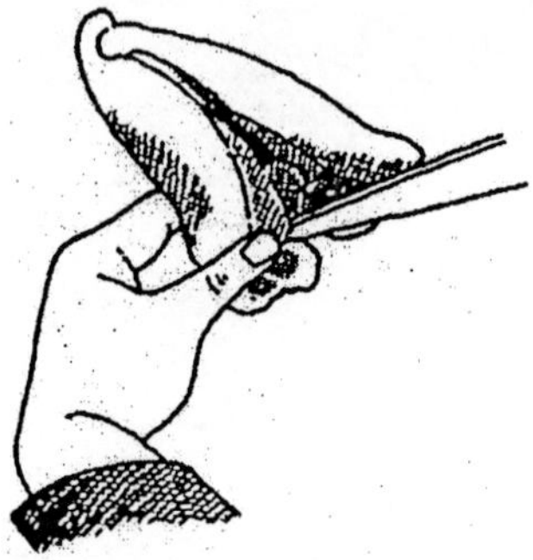

6.17. *Run the knife down the side of the carcuss against the bone and cut through the wing joint.*

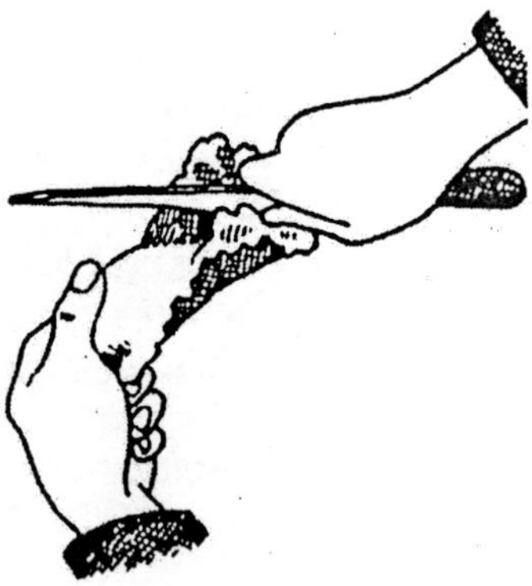

6.18. *Turn the bird on its side and pull the supreme off.*

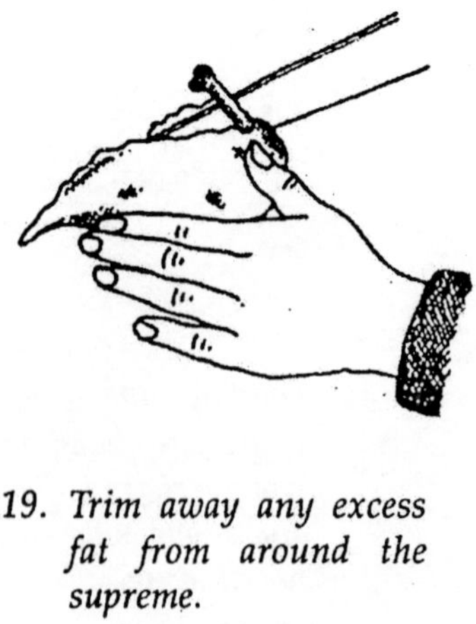

6.19. *Trim away any excess fat from around the supreme.*

TRUSSING A BIRD FOR ROASTING: METHOD 1

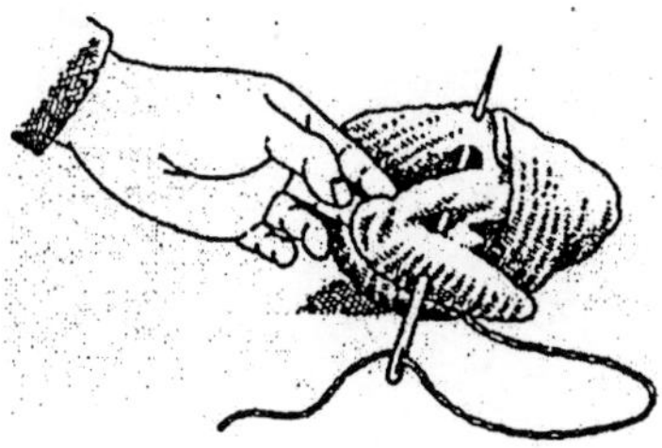

6.20. With the bird on its back, push the needle through between the two bones of the first part of the wing, over the bone on the next part and through the skin on the back.

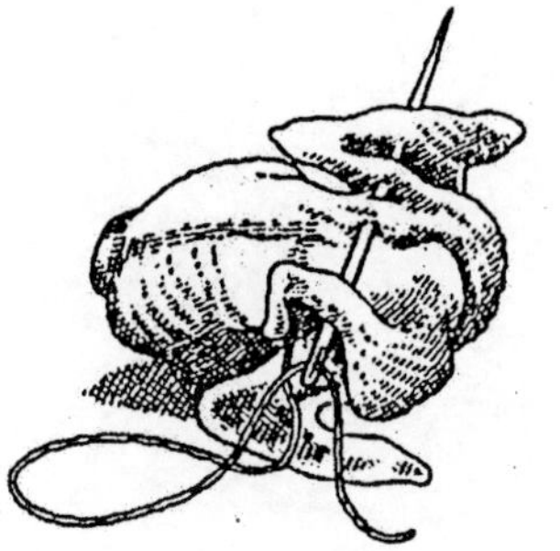

6.21. Push the needle through the neck flap, then repeat the process in reverse order for the other wing. Pull the string through.

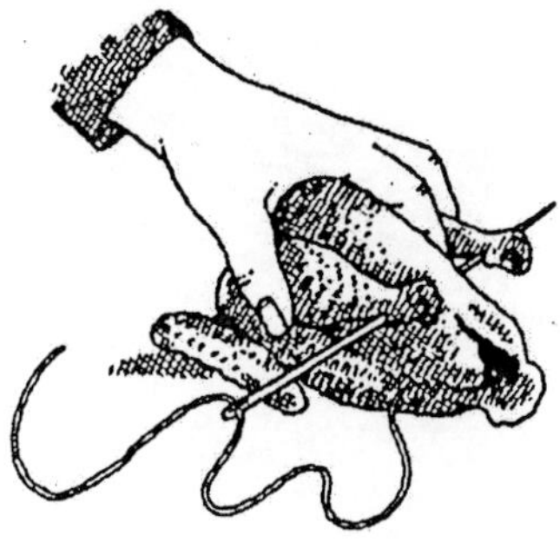

6.22. Turn the bird on to its back and push the trussing needle through the leg close to the joint at a-45 degree angle, coming out at the parson's nose end of the carcass on the opposite side of entry.

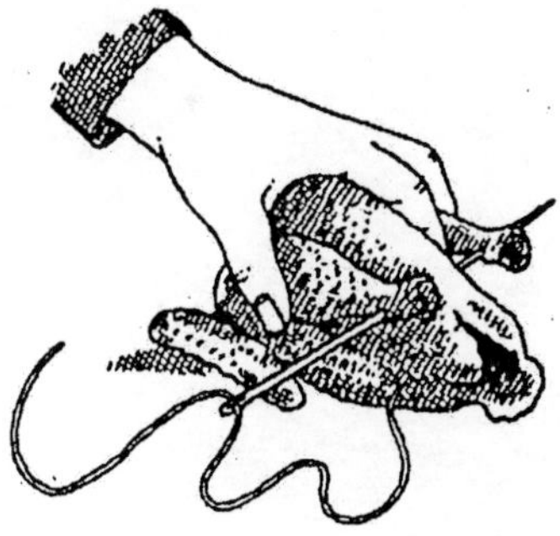

6.23. Pass the needle through the under the bone as close as possible to the top joint of the leg, pass the needle under the point of the breast bone and through the opposite leg.

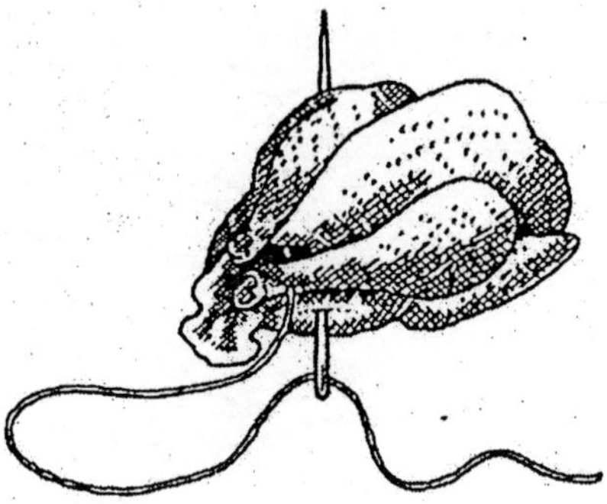

6.24. Push the needle through the carcass underneath the top leg joint at a 45 degree angle to come out beside the middle joint of the opposite leg.

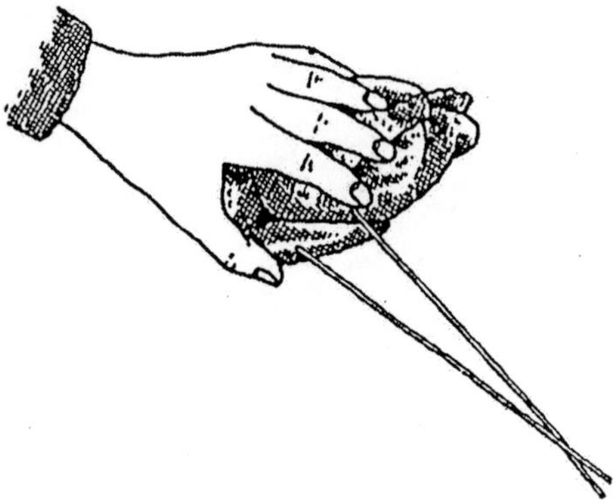

6.25. Pull both strings tight.

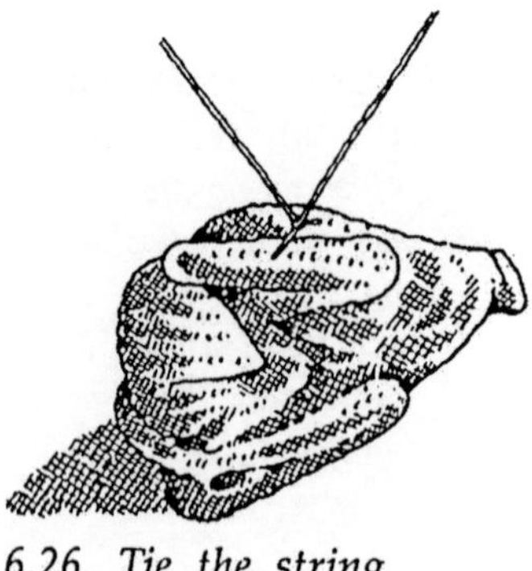

6.26. Tie the string.

TRUSSING A BIRD FOR ROASTING: METHOD 2

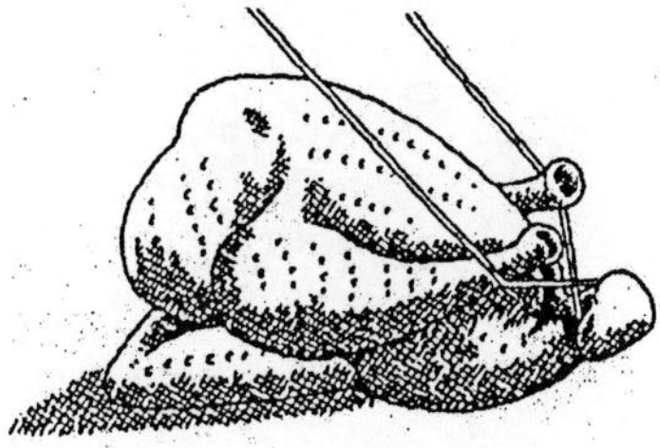

6.27. Pass the string under the parson's nose, then cross it over the top. Bring the string up both sides of the legs andcross it over.

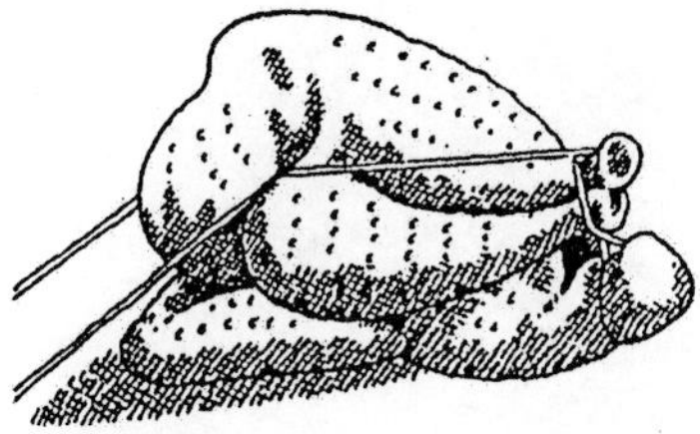

6.28. Pull the string tightly down between the legs and the breasts.

6.29. Bring the string over the top side of the wing bone and under the bird.

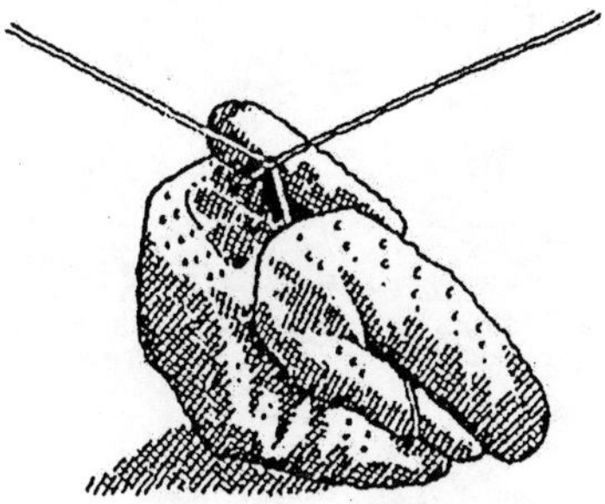

6.30. Tie the string off.

SKINNING A RABBIT OR HARE

6.31. Cut through the skin at the base of each leg.

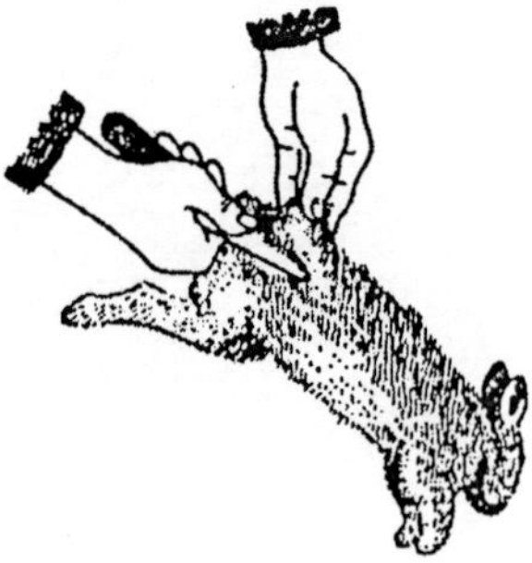

6.32. Cut the skin along the inside of the hind legs down to the belly and free the skin.

6.33. Cut through the tail.

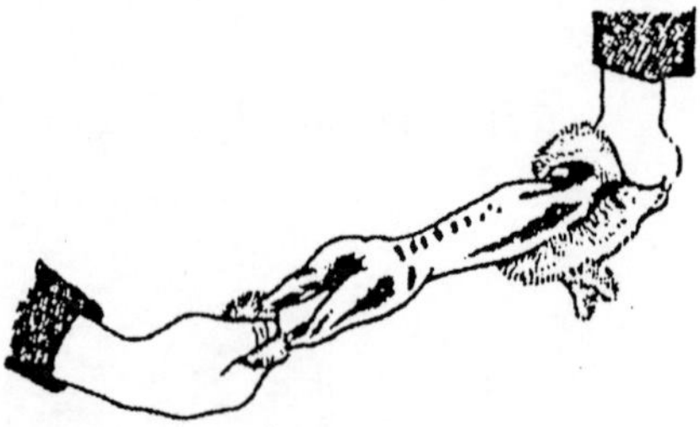

6.34. Holding the animal firmly by the back legs, pull off the skin towards the head using your free hand. Chop off the head.

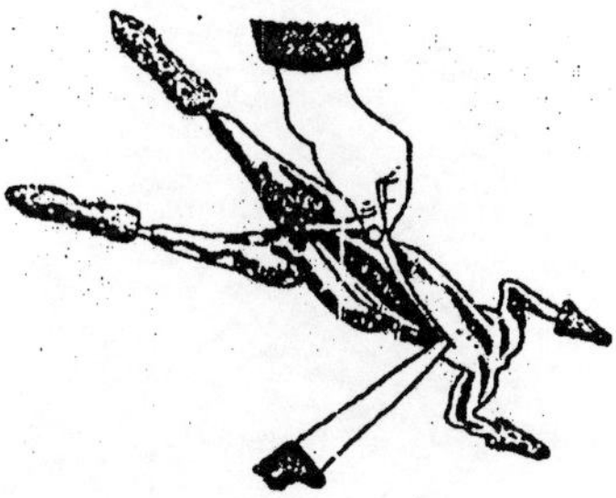

6.35. *Make an incision along the belly and remove the innards.*

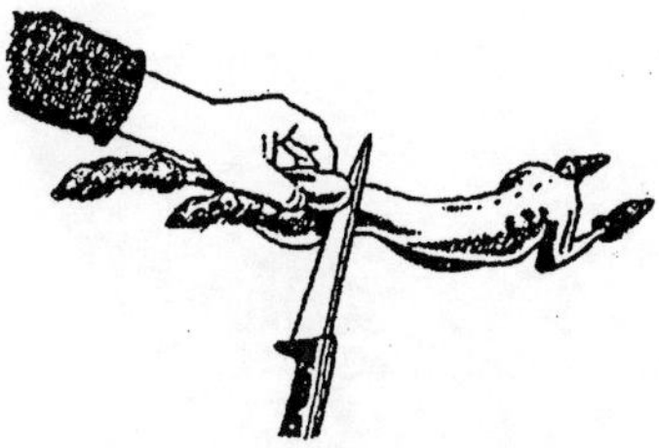

6.36. *At the base of the spine is a. 'V'-shaped bone (the pelvis.) Cut through the meat on the leg side of this bone down to the spine.*

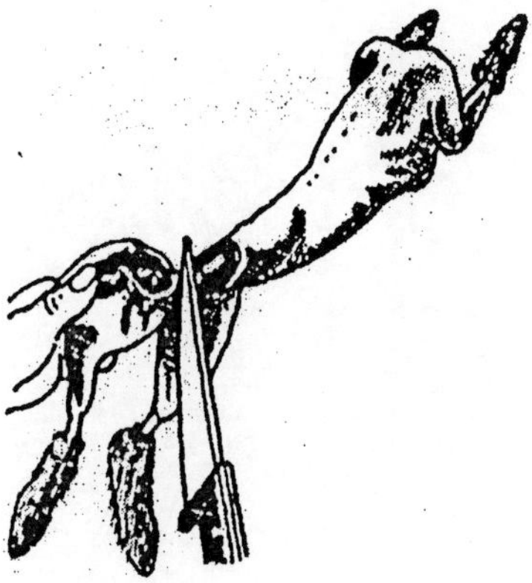

6.37. *Cut through the leg joint and remove the leg.*

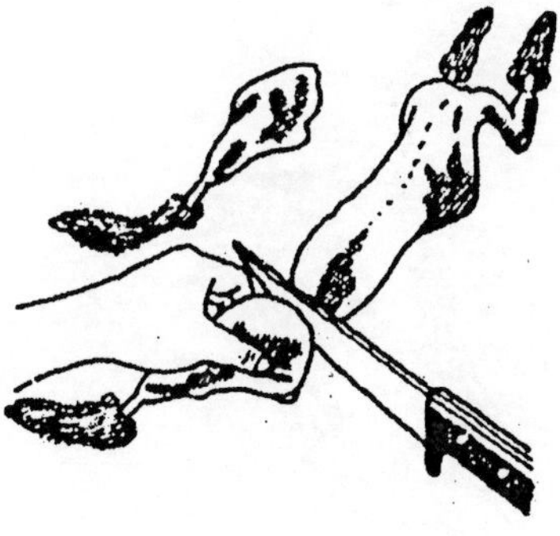

6.38. *Repeat on the other leg. Chop off the feet.*

6.39. *Cut off the front legs and chop off the feet.*

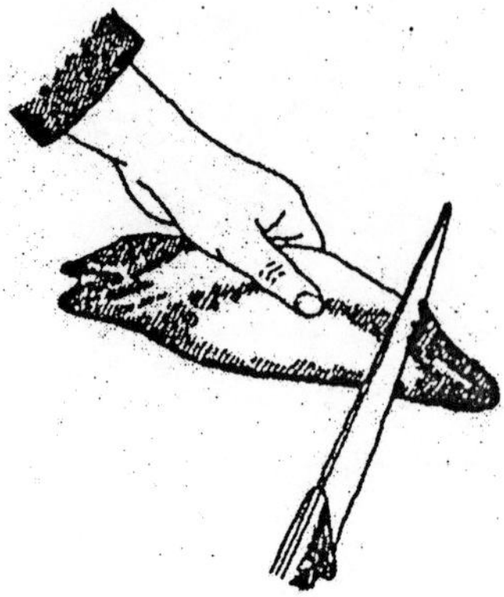

6.40. *Chope off the end of the carcass ons the saddle side of the pelvic bone.*

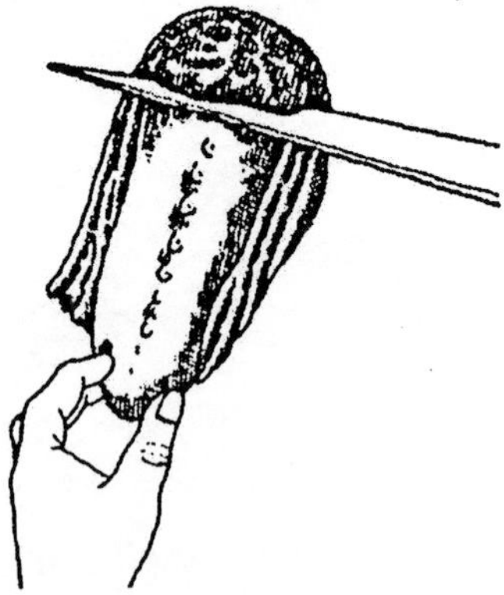

6.41. *Chop off the neck from the saddle.*

6.42. *Cut away the belly flap.*

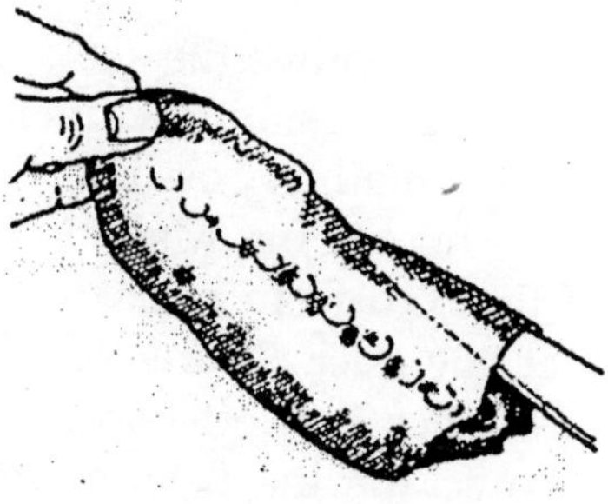

6.43. *Slide the knife under the sinew.*

6.44. *Cut away the sinew.*

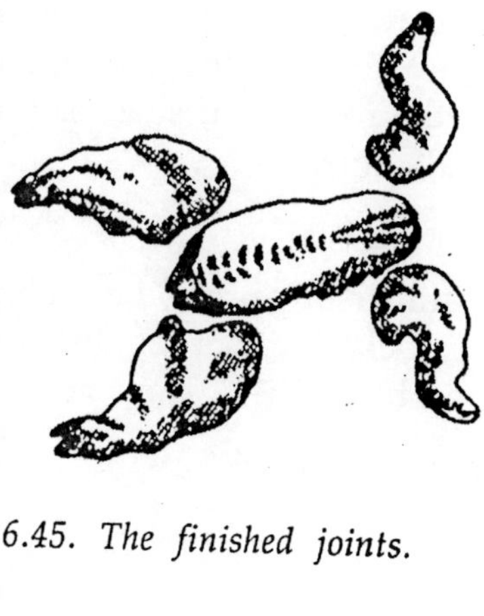

6.45. *The finished joints.*

Boning Out for Galantines

For this purpose it is necessary to remove the skeleton of the bird completely. Singe and draw the bird as usual, keeping the opening of the vent as small as possible. Cut of the winglet feet just below the hock joint. Make a cut along the centre of the back of the bird from neck to tail. Carefully remove the flesh over the back, lifting off the bones with the thumb and forefinger the left hand and using the tip of a small knife to scrape the flesh off the bone where necessary. On reaching the wings and thigh, find the joints and cut through the ligaments to detach them from the carcass. Continue towards the breast, carefully trimming away the fillets from the breastbone. Use the fingertips to raise the skin without tearing it. The thighs and drumsticks can now be boned out; leaving the knuckle of the hock attahed to the skin to contain the stuffing. Bone out the wing, channeling the bone from the winglet, stuff the bird as required, sew up the back, shape and truss.

Ballotine Preparation

These are small galantines made from the legs of chicken. After removing the leg from the carcass, remove the skin from the leg carefully to avoid tearing the skin. Leave the knuckle and approximately 2 cm of hock bone attached to the skin. With the flesh of the leg make forcemeat. Refill the skin with the forcemeat; sew up the opening and shape like a small horn.

DUCK

Duck is probably, the most universally praised member of the poultry family. The term duck, like that of chicken, covers many different types and qualities. They are:

1. Aylesbury Duck
2. Rouen
3. Nantes

4. Barbary
5. Long island

Buying Duck

Ducks are best when they are six-month old. To test the fat covering pinch the skin along the breast justs behind the legs. This will show how much fat the bird is carrying. The end of breastbone will always be pliable in a young bird and is the bird is young if hard then another bird. Soft flexible quills with a decided point are also a good indicator. The older the bird, the more rounded the tips. Cleaning and dressing are carried out as per the chicken.

GOOSE

Goose was considered the best of poultry in old England but now-a-days it is taken to be too greasy to eat or digest. The greatest claim to fame for the goose however has to be its liver—Foie gras—once known to be the "supreme fruit of gastronomy." Goose is best when they are still young, up to six months old, when they are known as Goslings or Green geese. Beyond one year of age the meat is good only for Braising. When choosing a goose, look for fine-grained pink flesh and a creamy white skin. The feet should be soft pliable and yellow. As the goose ages, the feet and bill becomes darker in colour.

GUINEA FOWL

Like quali, the guinea fowl is not strictly poultry. It is a semi-domesticated bird. It is a member of the pheasant family and originated in West Africa. The best age for guinea fowl is between 8 and 9 weeks.

TURKEY

Turkey has got the importance because of Christmas but in fact it is much more versatile bird than one can imagine. The best turkey is when it is 9 to 10 kg.

GAME LE GIBIER

The French word *gibier* applies to all animals being hunted and eaten. It is derived from the verb gibercer, which means, "to hunt". A lot of pleasure comes from the hunt that proceeds it to the pot, and the hunter takes the best himself. When choosing your game great care is needed. If you have shot the bird, yourself then freshness is not a problem. But if you are buying a bird from a game dealer, butcher or supermarket, a part from looking fresh, it should not have any unpleasant odour, and the skin, if the bird is plucked, should be dry, not mosit. If it is still in the feathers, then the eyes should be bright and not sunken and dull. All game should be hung before plucking, by the neck, in a cold dry place with plenty of space around each bird to allow the air to circulate freely. Do not hang the bird for more then 5 to 7 days. The age of the bird is also of great importance. A bird of one-year age will make very good eating, after that it starts becoming dry and tought.

Feathered Game

English	French
Pheasant	*Le faisan*
Partridge	*La perdrix*
Guinea fowl	*La pintade*
Quail	*La caille*
Plover	*Le pluvier*
Wild duck	*Le canard sauvage*
Grouse	*La grouse*
Mountain cock	*Le coq de brugere*
Snipe	La becassine
Wood cock	*La becasse*
Teal	*La sarcelle*

7

BUTCHERS MEATS

The butchery department, located in the gar de manger, uses the different types of meats like:—

(A) Beef which is known in French as BOEUF comes from BOVINAE family of animals like ox, cows and buffalos and veal called veau in French comes from the calf of cow and buffalo.

(B) Lamb and Mutton known in French as Agneau and mouton respectively comes from OVINAE family from animals like sheeps and goats.

(C) Pork becomes porc in French comes from SUDINAE family concerning pigs including both porker as well as gammon pigs.

Here I would like to give a brief on slaughtering technqiues because it directly affects the quality of meats. In India we are in the process of improving the hygienic standards in slaughtering techniques to bring the meat at par with the international standards.

SLAUGHTERING TECHNIQUES

(A) Ante mortem inspection

A medical checkup of the animal is conducted to check whether the animal is suffering from any contagious disease like tuberculosis, typhoid, gaestro enteritis etc. Body temperature should be 101.4° F while ears hoofs and horn should be cool to touch. The eyes should be clear, the animal should be alert. It should attempt to move away when approached. The skin should be mellow to touch and freely moving on the underside. There should of course be no bare patches or signs of parasitic conditions. The breathing should be steady and regular. The muzzle should be moist. The animal should be viewed from the side and in beef types should present a straight back. The body generally rectangular in form. A coarse tail frequently indicates a big boned animal.

(B) Fasting

Minimum 24 hours fasting is necessary. The fasting pan should be cool and clean. Plenty of water should be available. This will insure minimum intestinal content consequently less chance of bacterial contamination. The fasting will also prevent the blood system goged with partly assimilated food substances, which are known to effect the condition of beef. Nervous excitement and physical exertion should be avoided, as it will result in rise of body temperature, which will cause imperfect bleeding. Excessive muscle faltigue will mean that glycogen of the muscle is used up and while slaughtering, it changes into lactic acid. Excessive acidity causes bone sour.

(C) Roping

With bow-line knot round the neck care should be taken that windpipe may not get choked.

(D) Stunning

Except KOSHER slaughtering animals are rendered unconscious by the following methods:

(1) Knocking with a 4-lb sledgehammer it results is very effective bleeding.

Note: while stunning care should be taken that the medulla oblongata should be intact.

(2) Striking with a bullet or a blank cartridge.

(3) A leather mask, which is equipped with a bolt to, struck at the right place with a hammer.

(4) Electrical stunning 60 to 80 volt low voltage high frequency current is given. It is difficult in case of cows and buffaloes. Generally goats and sheeps are electrically stunned.

(5) **Gas:** Carbon monoxide is used to stun the pigs prior to slaughter.

STICKING

The object of bleeding is to remove the blood as completely and rapidly as possible. Blood is an ideal medium for bacterial growth. An incision is made just in front of sternum cutting into the main blood vessels. The cut should be made by making the animals lying on its side and not while hoisting the animal upside down as there will be pressure on the organs.

DRESSING

The slaughterman places one foot in front of the fore legs and the other foot below the head so that the skin of the throat is tight. The end of brisket is located and an incision is made from just in front of brisket on the centerline of the neck towards the head. The thymus is removed. The knife directed towards the point of the brisket and by moving it in the direction of the backbone the blood vessels are cut just outside the chest cavity.

The blood drain from the body is assisted by pumping the foreleg. The animal is scalped by chopping off the horns and the head is skinned out, generally by a junior. A cut is made across the throat and windpipes tied off, the head is detached by cutting through the muscle and the joint (occipital). The front legs are jointed leaning the knucklebones on the carcass. The hide is sometime removed from them. The hind legs are jointed by cutting through the tendons so that the toes will fall forward. The slaughterman grabs a foot in between his legs and a cut is made down the hide over the round to point just behind the udder or cod fat.

FLAYING

A rip is then made from the incisions caused by sticking in a straight line over the brisket along the middle line of the belly to the tail. The hide is removed from the neck and brisket. Some slaughtermen leave the hide on the knuckles. The process is carried out in long and firm strokes until the hide is within six inches from the floor. At this stage the caracass is wiped with clean hot cloth. The abdominal cavity is opened up and the cannal fat is removed. The bladder emptited and viscera pushed to one side so that the buttocks can be split up. The brisket is cut down to the bone and sawn through. The food and wind pipes are loosened. The hide over tail is removed and then from round and rump. After this the caracass is hoisted up and the weight of the intestine and stomach with spleen attached sufficient to remove them. Then liver is removed by cutting through the attachment with diaphragm. Then the pluck is removed from the chest cavity.

The remaining blood vessels from the throat and chest are trimmed out and then the side of the caracass is wiped with clean warm towel. Then the backbone is first cut into two and the sides are separated.

HEAD

The tongue is loosened from the sides and then cut from the back and removed. It is cleaned and pickled.

Then the lower jaw is loosened and sawed through the bone to separate it from the upper jaw. The cheek meat is carefully removed and brain is also removed. The lips can be minced and are used for making the stock.

PLUCK

The pluck in ox consists of tracheas, lung and heart.

Heart

The outer cover of heart pericardium is cut through and heart is removed by cutting through the blood vessel. Extra blood is squeezed out and the heart is hung to cool.

Lungs

If lungs are to be used then a careful examination is made to check if there are any blood patches or food particles in them or not. They are pumped cleaned and then hung to cool.

Stomachs

The cow has four stomachs. The stomachs should not be opened at the slaughtering time, as there are chances of contamination in the caracass. The third and the fourth stomachs known "omasum" and "abomasum" are detached and the two are separated. Normally the third stomach [bible bag] is disposed off intact. The fourth stomach known as rennet or reed can be considered edible is opened up well washed. The first and second stomachs [paunch and honeycomb] are emptied off their contents and washed thoroughly. Washing is done with water at 140°F.

Cowheels: The hairs are removed by blanching as used for stock making.

Sweetbreads: They are known as Thymus present in the throat or Pancreas. In the younger animal thymus is used as sweetbread while in the older animals pancreas is used as thymus. In French it is called 'RIS' and weighs about 700 to 800 grams.

Intesting: Large and small intestines of cows are used for the manufacture of sausages.

Beef Fats: The quantity of fat depends upon the weight and finish of the animal.

OFFAL

1. **Ox cheeks and head trimmings:** stewing BRAWN and sausage making.
2. **Tongue:** salting and boiling.
3. **Brain:** Boiling, sauce and sausage making.
4. **Sweetbreads:** frying and boiling.
5. **Heart:** baking boiling or sausage making.
6. **Liver:** frying.
7. **Spleen:** pie making and falvouring soups.
8. **Tail:** soups and stews making.
9. **Kidneys:** stewing, frying and soup making.
10. **Blood:** black pudding sausage.
11. **Stomach:** cleaned and boiled for tripe.
12. **Feet:** stock preparation.
13. **Fats:** suet for pudding and paste for mincemeat, beef fat for drippings.
14. **Bones:** preparation of soups and manufacture of gelatin.

BEEF DISSECTION OR BUTCHERY CUTS

The full carcass is to be cut in two lengthwise pieces by sawing through the backbone. It will separate the carcass in two sides. Then each side is to be cut through wing rib and fore rib giving two quarters known as fore quarter and hindquarter.

CARCASS CUTS

English Name	French Name	Weight	Uses
Shin	La jambe	7 kg	Consomme beef tea stewing
Top side	La tranche tender	10 kg	Braising stewing, 2nd class roasting
Silver side	La gite a la noix	14 kg	Brine pickling & boiling
Thick flank	La tranche grasse	2 kg	Braising and stewing
Rump	La culotte de boeuf	10 kg	Grilling frying and steak making
Sirloin frying	L'aloyau de boeuf	9 kg	Roasting grilling and steack making
Wingrib frying	La cote de boeuf	5 kg	Roasting grilling and steak making
Thinflank	La bavette	10 kg	Stewing boiling and sausage making
Fillet	Le filet de boeuf	3 kg	Roasting grilling frying and steak making
FORE QUARTER			
Forerib	Les cotes	8 kg	Roasting and braising
Middle ribe	Les cotes	10 kg	Roasting and braising
Chuckrib	Les cotes du collier	15 kg	Stewing and brasing
Sticking piece	La collier	10 kg	Stewing and sausage making
Plate	La poitrine	20 kg	Stewing and sausage making
Brisket	La poitrine	19 kg	Brine pickled and boiled also pressed beef
Leg of mutton cut	La tallon du collier	11 kg	Braising and stewing
Shank	La jambe	6 kg	Consomme and beef tea
Beef bones	Les os		
Bone marrow	La moelle		

BEEF|CUTS

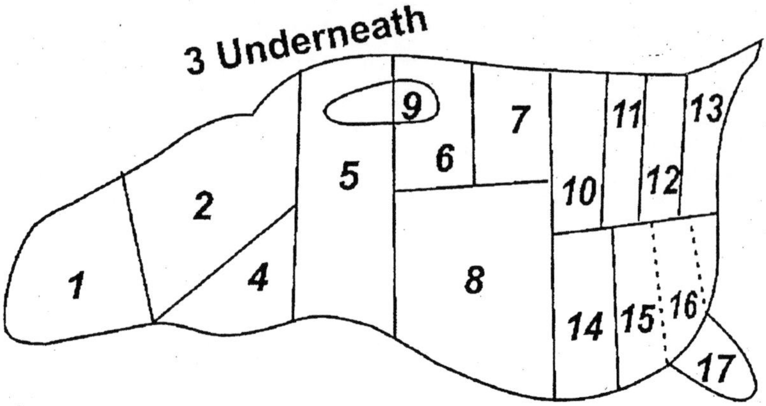

Fig. 7.1: Weight 180 kg Beef Cuts

Method of Dissection

1. Forequarter

The forequarter is placed on the cutting board with bone down and the joint of humerous is searched with the backward and down movement of shin with the help of the boning knife the shin is removed by cutting trough the joint. Then the sticking piece is removed by one straight cut from the humerous end of the ball end of the bone then continuing across the quarter to the back. The ball and socket joint is completely opened then the sticking piece is removed. After that the plate and brisket are dissected by sawing along the fore rib. The eye of the meat at the forerib is measured and twice that measurement the cut is given along the fore rib then plate and brisket are removed and separated. Then from brisket the leg of mutton cut is made with sticking piece, plate and brisket removed. The forequarter is called by pony or rib or crop.

To dissect the crop it is turned over with flesh downwards and the tip of flesh along the back bone is removed then with the help of sawing machine a cut is made through second and third ribe from neck with this leg of mutton cut, chuck and blade bone are removed. Then fore rib and middle rib are removed by giving four ribs to each joint.

Hindquater

Remove the kidney knob. Remove rump and loin from the leg [thick flank, silver side, topside]. Remove fillet separate rump and loin. Then divide the leg in joints.

Separate hindquarter and forequarter by cutting through 10th and 11th rib leaving three ribs on the hind and ten ribs on the forequarter.

Nomenclature of Animals Intended for Beef

1. **Bull calf:** immature entire male one year old.
2. **Bull:** matured entire male one year old.
3. **Steers:** castrated male one year old.
4. **Heifer:** young immature female up to one year old, which has not reproduced.
5. **Cow:** Matured female over one year old which has reproduced.

Preparation of Beef Cuts

1. **Shin:** The cut is to be boned around the leg bone then remove excess fat, sinews. It will be good use for clarification, beef tea, and inferior mince.
2. **Top Side:** This is one of the leanest cut of whole beef. It is tender and has got many uses like making stews or braised steaks.
3. **Silver Side:** The meat in this cut is very coarse and needs a long cooking time. The popular method preserving in brine and boiling. It can be served as cold meats for salads and sandwiches.

4. **Thick Flank:** This is also a lean and tender cut of meat and because of its tenderness it's used for braised steaks and stews.
5. **Rump:** The rump is carefully boned out of the hipbone and excess fat and sinews are removed. This is rarely used, as a roast popular use for this cut is rumpsteak.
6. **Sirloin:** The true sirloin consists of fillet and sirloin. The filet should be removed very carefully. The sirloin can be roasted on the bone or de-bone sirloin called contrefilet and then neatly sliced into portions. Contrefilet can also be used as entrecote minute, entrecote and entrecote double steak.
7. **Wingrib:** This joint has got three rib bones and is the first class joint for roasting.
8. **Think Flank:** This cut has got coarse meat qualities and also lot of fat and can be used for boiling, stewing and mincing, after removal of the fat.
9. **Filet:** This is the most tender joint in the whole beef and taken as the prime cut. There are very famous steaks prepared from this joint.
   (a) **Chateaubriand Steak:** This from the head of the filet. Its three to ten cm thick and weighs to 300 g to 1 kg. Serving for 2 to 4 persons.
   (b) **Filet Stake:** approximately four steaks each of one and a half to two cm thickness, with weight to 100 to 150 grams.
   (c) **Toumedos:** Approximately six to eight steaks each weighing 100 grams, with thickness of 2 to 4 cm.
   (d) **Filet Mignon:** This is the tail of the filet left after cutting the above steaks.

   The whole filet is cleaned excess fat and sinews removed and then roasted whole or can be pot-roasted also (poeling).

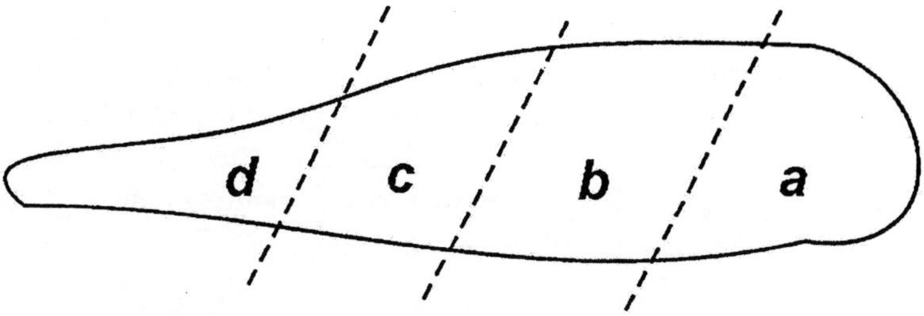

Fig. 7.2

10. **Forerib**: This is a very good cut from the forequarter and consists of our ribs. The chine bone is cut into two to three places and excess fat and sinews removed. Before roasting the back flat chin bone should be broken with the back of a chopper. The cut can be de-bone like the sirloin and can be roasted without bone or cut into stakes for kosher cooking.
11. **Middlerib**: Deboned remove the sinews and cut into smaller pieces tie with a sting and used for roasting or brazing.
12. **Chuckrib**: This is generally boned out and either cut into dices for stewing or into slices for brazing steaks.
13. **Sticking Piece**: This is the neck of the beef and got lean meat around the neck bone. Deboned cut into dices or minced for stew or mince meat.
14. **Brisket**: This is a popular cut from the forequarter which is deboned, rolled, brined and boiled and served as a pressed beef.
15. **Plate:**—Boned and cut into dices for stews or used for minced beef.
16. **Leg of Mutton Cut**: This is a good quality lean meat piece deboned and is used as dices for stews or as slices for brazing steaks.

17. **Shank:** The shank is carefully boned around the leg bone and very tough sinews and excess fat are removed. It can be cut into large cubes or minced for clarification of stockes or in the preparation of beef tea. It can also be used in large dices in the preparation of goulash stew.
18. **Fat (la glaisse):** The kidney fat, i.e. suet and cod fat is used for making the stuffing's while all other fats are used as drippings.
19. **Bones:** The knucklebones are sawn and split to remove the bone marrow and then it's washed with cold water to remove excess blood. The marrow can be used in the preparation of sauces and soups, while the bones are used for stocks.

Veal **le Veau**

This meat is from the calf, which are two and half to three months old. It is only fed on milk and its meat should be white with a slight tinge of green. The meat is lean very little fat is visible around the kidneys and it has got the pleasant smell of milk.

Veal is sold in full caracass like lamb or mutton. It is generally split into two halves like the beef carcass. Then its further cut into the various cuts as illustrated below:

Veal Cuts

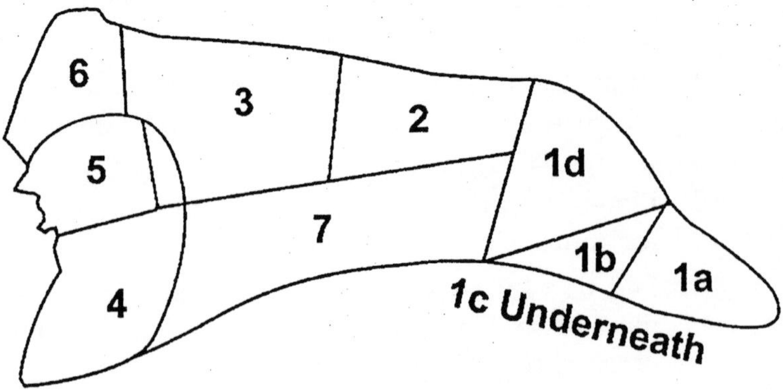

Fig. 7.3

English Name	French Name	Weight	Use
Leg	Le cuissot de Veau	10 kg	Stewing, roasting, sauteing and braising.
Loin	La long de veau	6 kg	Roasting, frying and grilling.
Best-end	Le carre de veau	6 kg	Roasting, frying and grilling.
Shoulder	L'epaule de veau	10 kg	Braising and stewing
Neck-end	Le cou de veau	3 kg	Stewing
Scrag	Le cou de veau	2 kg	Stewing and stock
Breast	La poitrine de veau	3 kg	Stewing and roasting
Leg of veal			
• Thick flank	La quasi	3.5 kg	Escalopes, roasting, sauteing and braising.
• Under	La sous noix	3 kg	Escalopes, roasting,
cushion	La noix de veau	3 kg	sauting and braising.
• Knuckle	Le jarret de veau	1.5 kg	Stewing.

Lamb and Mutton **L'agneau 'Et Le Mouton**

The sketch shown below illustrates the various cuts of lamb and mutton but before that let us understand the difference between lamb and mutton. Lamb is from goat or sheep, which is less than one year old while mutton, come from goat or sheep, which is more than a year old.

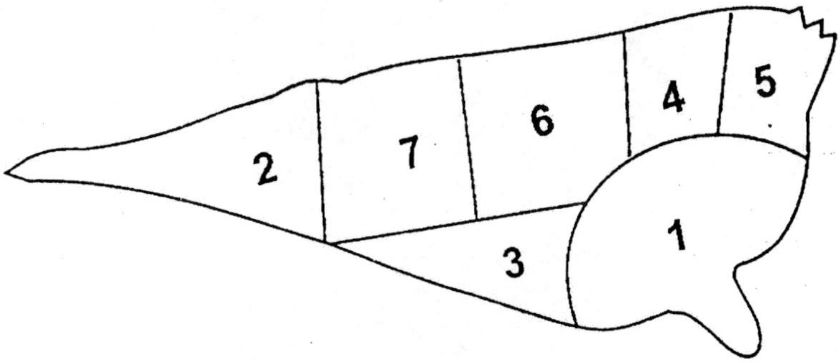

Fig. 7.4

Best End and Saddle

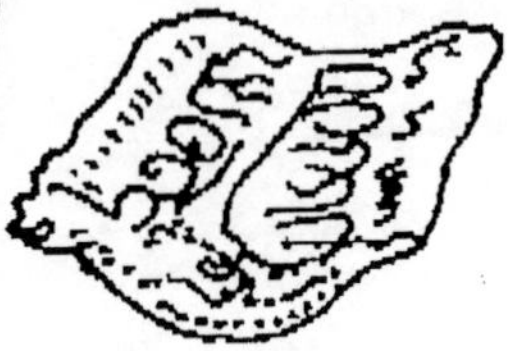

Saddle

Best End

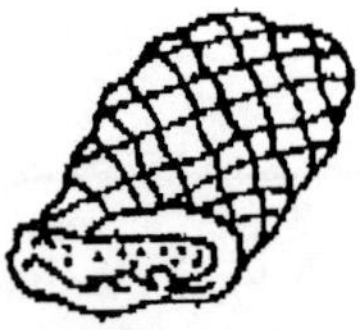

Normal Saddle (Prep. for Rosting)

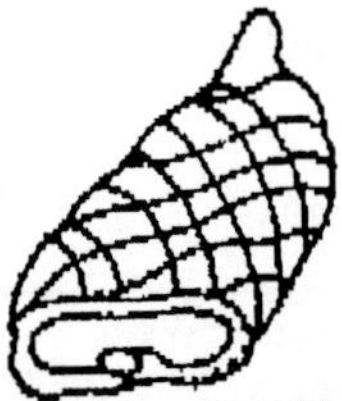

Long Saddle (Prep. for Rosting)

Deboned Loin

Loin of Lamb

Loin for Roasting on Bones

Loin for Roasting

Chop

Boned Loin for cutting

Noissettes

Rosette of Lambs cut from boned saddle

English Name	French Name	Weight Forlamb	Weight for Mutton	Uses
Shoulder	Lepaule d' agneau ou de mouton	3 kg	4.5 kg	Roasting and stewing
Leg	Le gigot	3.5 kg	5.5 kg	Roasting and boiled mutton
Breast	Piotrine	1.5 kg	2.5 kg	Stewing and roasting
Middle neck	Le cou	2.5 kg	3 kg	Stewing
Scrag end	Le cou	0.5 kg	1 kg	Broth
Best end	Le carre	2 kg	3 kg	Roasting grilling and frying
Saddle	La salle	3.5 kg	5.5 kg	Roasting grilling and frying
Cutlet	La cotelette			Grilling and frying

Loin or la longe is obtained by dissecting the saddle into two halves.

Cutlet is obtained by cutting the middle neck or best end along the ribs bone in to six single cutlets or three double cutlets.

Slicing the loin into six equal pieces across the backbone makes Lamb chop or mutton chop.

Dissection of Carcass

1. Remove the shoulder by incising at a point where the shoulder bulges at the neck and along the back to a point between the 6th and 7th ribs, where the cartilage of the top of the bladebone can be easily cut through; the shape of the shoulder can be round or square.
2. Now cut along the rib bone to a point parallel with elbow.

3. Now curve the cut two-inch below the elbow and join with the starting point.
4. With the help of a boning knife cut through the seam between the neck muscle and shoulder and separate the shoulder.
5. Remove the legs by cutting through the aitchbone.
6. Remove the breasts by taking a point one-inch below the neck and sawing through the ribe bones in a straight line.
7. Remove the saddle by cutting through the cartilage between 12th and 13th vertebrae.
8. Separate the best ends by cutting through the 6th and 7th vertebrae and saw through the bone.
9. Now separate middle neck and scrag end by cutting through the cervical vertebrae and 1st dorsal vertebrae.

PREPARTION OF CUTS

1. Legs

The leg joint is cleaned with extra fat removed. Then removes the aitchbone piece by cutting through the ball and socket joint. Now remove the knucklebone. Take the meat from the leg bone towards the centre to around three-inch along the bone and tie the whole joint with a string. This is called a French leg. This process is done before the roasting method.

2. Best end

For roasting, cut on either side of backbone through fat and meat. Now remove the backbone completely. Remove fat and sinews and cut through the ribs at an angle. For preparing cutlets cut between each rib evenly to get single or double cutlets.

3. Saddle

The whole roasted saddle is used for cold buffet, skin the saddle and cut through about one inch of flap on both the sides, remove kidney and excess fat then tie neatly with a string. For making chops or noisettes cut through the backbone in to even size pieces.

4. Breast

For roasting, remove excess fat and skin, bone stuff and roll, tie with a string.

5. Shoulder

For roasting, clean and trim the knuckle bone and remove the blade bone by cutting through the ball joint with a boning knife and draw away with a duster. Now remove the arm bone. Stuff, roll and tie with a string.

Al'anglaise stuffing for mutton or lamb.

50 grams of suet

50 grams of cooked chopped onions

1 eggs

100 grams white bread crumbs

Little powdered thyme

Chopped parsley

Seasoning to taste

Method:—combine all to taste.

Pork **Le Porc**

Breeding the pigs in two different styles generates the pork meat. The pigs required for the preparation of bacon are called gammons, are given extra fatty diet and lot of rest so that the pigs acquire a lot of fat while the pigs required for the production of ham or pork meat commonly known as porker pigs are given a special diet rich in herbs but lacking in fats. The slaughtering technique for pigs includes gassing for stunning because the animal is thick skinned.

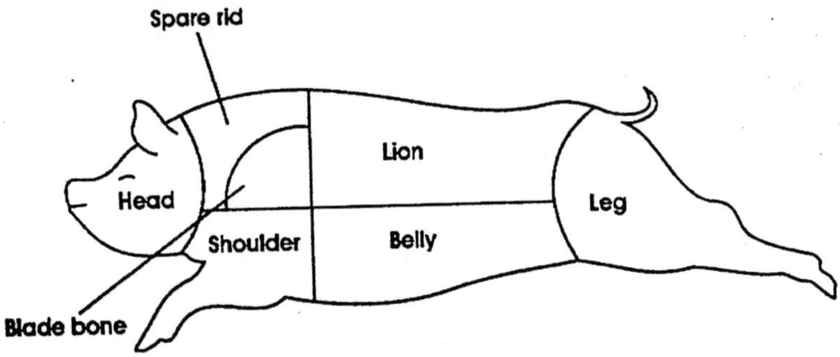

Fig. 7.6: Cuts of Pork

English Name	French Name	Weight	Uses
Leg	Le cuissot de porc	10 kg	Roasting and boiling
Loin	La longe de porc	8 kg	Roasting frying and grilling
Spare rib	La basse cote	5 kg	Roasting and pie making
Belly	La poitrine	5 kg	Pickling and boiling
Shoulder	L'epaule de porc	8 kg	Roasting sausages and pies
Head	La tete	2 kg	Brawn

BACON, GAMMON AND HAMS

Bacon

This comes from the baconer pig. This pertains to the fatty part of pork.

Bacon can be boned cut into rashers and salt cured or brine cured, it can be smoked or can be green bacon.

Cuts of Bacon

English name	weight	Use
Hock of gammon	2 kg	Boiling
Middle of gammon	3 kg	Grilling and Frying
Corner of gammon	2 kg	Grilling and Frying
Back-bacon	4 kg	Grilling and Frying
Thick end of back	3 kgms	Frying and boiling
Collar	4 kgms	Boiling
Fore hock	4 kgms	Boiling
Best streaky	4 kgms	Griling and Frying
Thin streaky	2 kgms	Griling and Frying
Flank	1.5 kgms	Boiling and Frying

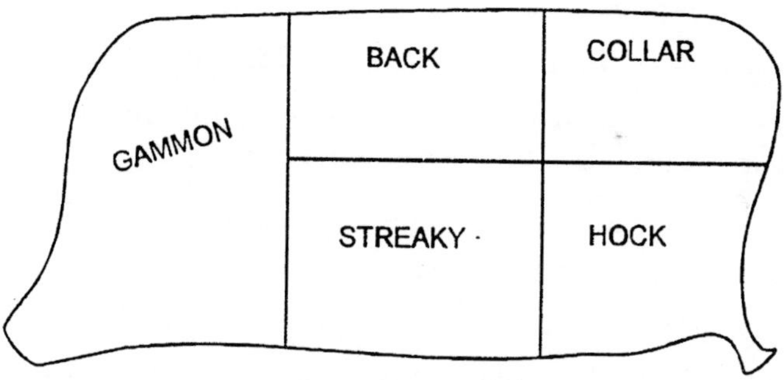

Fig. 7.7: Side of Bacon

Gammon

Gammon is the hind leg of baconer pig. It can be green or smoked and is suitable for boiling, braising and baking. It can be served hot or cold. The best known gammons are Danish and Wiltshire. For the gammon boiled and cold, place the gammon in a pan and boil in fresh cold water, skim and simmer for about half an hour and leave it to cool in its own cooking liquor. Clean it nicely and cover with mustard and browned breadcrumbs and carve it and serve.

Hams

Ham is the hind part of the leg of porker pig and mainly processed in three ways:

1. It is cured in brine, smoked, dried and cooked served hot or cold example glazed ham and hamburger schinken.
2. These are dry or wet cured hams, smoked, hung to dry and always served raw. Example: Bayonne ham, Westphallian ham and Toulouse ham.
3. Dry or wet cured hams which are matured and then cooked and served hot or cold. Example: York ham and Parma ham.

Popular Hams

Westphallian ham **Jambon d'Allemagne**

This is the best ham, which is eaten raw mostly served as appetizer.

French ham **Jambon de Bayonne**

This ham is eaten raw in thin slices.

Italian ham **Jambon d'Italie**

Parma is most popular among hams. This is also eaten raw.

English hams **Jambon d' Angleterre**

These are very dark colour hams. They are wet cured and smoked. Can be served hot or cold.

Danish hams **Jambon Danois**

Here the curing starts while the pigs are still alive because they are fed on special diet. They can be smoked or green and can be served hot or cold.

American hams **Jambon d' Amerique**

These hams are mostly green and wet cured in brine. They can be served hot or cold. They are slightly sweet because of the presence of molasses while curing.

Brief Note on Charcuterie

Charcuterie is the art of transforming pork into various preparations, an array of dishes, which have traditionally held a very important place in Gastronomy.

Charcuterie

Names of some pork products are given below:

English name	French name
White pudding	Bouding Blanc
Blood pudding	Bouding Noir
Sausage meat	Chair a saucisse
Small Sausages	Chipolatas
Sausage in Pork caul	Crepinettes
Pork Forcemeat	Farce de Pore
Boiled Ham	Jambon Blanc de Paris
Mortadella	Mortadelle
Pork Liver Pate	Pate de Foie de Porc
Roast Pork in Aspic	Roti de Porc Pique
Frankfurters	Saucisses de Frankfort
Dry Salami	Saucisses Secs

This trade is very old, under strict control as far back as the 10th century. On 17th of January 1475, the first formal statues were organized for charcuterie by Robert D' Estouville, who was in charge of establishing the community of charcutiers in the town of Paris. Later on

18th of July 1513, a royal verdict by King Louis the 12th, authorized the charcutiers to slaughter pigs bought anywhere in the kingdom, and to prepare the meats to the liking of their customers. It appears that after that date, charcuterie became officially known as Masters preparing and selling raw meat and delicacies. A few examples of dishes and their recipes will help in developing skills in charcuterie.

Soft Brine (Brine Cure, Curing Brine)Saumure Douce

4 litres	Water
½ kg	Salt
120 g	Curing Salt
30 g	Sugar
1 sm. bag	filled with Bay leaves, thyme, peppercorn, juniper berries, basil, ginger, marjoram, sage:

Method

(1) Combine all ingredients.

(2) Boil aproximately three minutes, stirring frequently, until the salts and sugar are dissolved.

(3) Cool, strain through a cheesecloth.

This mixture must be thoroughly chilled before it is ready for use.

Sausage Meat **Chair a Saucisse**

2.5 kg	Skinless and boneless pork butts
60 g	salt
1pinch	curing salt
¼ tsp.	Ground black pepper

Method

(1) Spread seasonings over the meat.

(2) Grind coarsely; mix in a blender, slowly adding water (about ½ pint or less).

(3) Refrigerate finished product until needed.

Pork Forcemeat **Farce de Porc**

1 kg	Lean white pork meat
750 g	Fatback
30 g	Salt
¼ tsp.	Pepper (ground, white)
1 pinch	pate spice
1 sm. pinch	Nutmeg
1	Egg white

Method

Puree meat and spices in a blender, adding the egg white slowly.

This mixture may be used in galantines and ballotines.

NOTE: For any pate or galantine or ballotine requiring forcemeat, the forcemeat will have to be made with the small parts of the meat of the animal, keeping the best pieces to be marinated in the usual manner, using the wine or liquor indicated in the recipe and the same amount of pork fat.

BREAKFAST SAUSAGE

4 kg	Pork (1/3 fat– 2/3 lean)
15 g	Ground White Pepper
60 g	Salt
10 g	seasoning
750 ml.	very cold water

ITALIAN STYLE SAUSAGE

4.5 kg	Pork (25% fat, 75% lean)
30 g	Coarse ground black pepper

90 g	Salt
5 g	Paprika
30 g	Whole Fennel Seeds
500 ml.	Cold water

FRENCH STYLE GARLIC SAUSAGE

1 kg	Lean beef
1 kg	Pork Butts (22%–25% fat)
20 g	Salt
3 g	curing salt
1 tsp	Ground white pepper
10 g	Finely chopped fresh garlic
120 g	Potato starch
300 ml	Cold Water
½ tsp	M.S.G.
½ kg	Fresh pork fatback, cut into neat 1/8 in. dices

Polish Style Sausage Kielbasi

5 lb.	Pork butt (fresh)
1½ oz	Salt
½ oz	Sugar
1/3 oz	Coarse ground black pepper
1¼ tsp	Crushed coriander seeds
3/4 oz	Fresh garlic (mashed fine)
6 oz.	Very cold water
1/8 oz.	Curing Salt

Merguez Sausage

3 kg	Lean beef
3 kg	Breast of lamb

20 g	Salt (per kilo) (Total 120 grams)
3 Tblasp.	Ground Black pepper
1 tsp.	Cayenne pepper
1 tsp.	Ground red pepper
10 g	Finely pureed garlic
1 tsp.	Ground cumin (comino)
5 tblsp.	Tomato paste
½ can	Harissa (2 ozs.)
1 liter	water (approximate)

Method

Cube all beef in 2 inch cubes. Bone the breast of lamb (it should not be too fatty); cube it. Mix all cubed meat and rest of ingredients, except water. Grind meat grinder. Mix in water, pack in sheep casings, twist 5″ long. Sausages are ready to be panfried or barbequed.

Blood Sausage **Boundin Noir**

½ gal	Blood (preferably pigs' blood)
1 lb.	Leaf lard
10 lb	Onions, diced
1 qt.	Heavy cream
	Salt, pepper
1 tbsp.	Pâté Spice
	Pork casing
½ lb	Butter

Method

(1) Remove skin from and dice leaf lard.

(2) Smother onions well in butter, cool add leaf lard.

(3) Add all other ingredients (exc. casings), stirring carefully when book in introduced.

(4) Using a funnel, fill casings and twist to desired size.

(5) Drop sausages into boiling water, lowering the heat immediately to prevent bursting.

(6) Using a small pot or ladle, keep the simmering water in motion.

(7) Cook the sausages for about 25 minutes.

(8) Using a needle or toothpick, pierce one sausage; if no blood comes out, the Sausages are ready.

(9) Remove from water and lay on sheet pans; lined with side towels.

Small Sausages **Chipolatas**

Sausage meat

Lamb casing

Method

(1) Soak and rinse thoroughly the lamb casings.

(2) Stuff meat in casings, twist to about 2½".

(3) Use in rabbit stew or any other dish requiring chipolatas.

Make Toulouse Sausage (Saussine De Toulouse) the same way, only use pork casing and twist to approximately 6″ long.

Frankfurters **Saucisses de Frankfort**

2 lb	Lean pork meat
3½ oz.	Iced water
3/4 oz.	Salt
1 pinch	Curing salt
1½ tsp.	Ground white pepper
1 pinch	Mixed spices
1 small pinch	Ground cumin

1	Lemon, juice of lamb casings

Method

(1) Grind meat, salt, and curing salt together, refrigerate for 2 hours.

(2) Place in blender; and iced water slowly; add seasoning and lemon juice.

(3) Stuff into lamb castings dry for 3 hours in drying room; cold smoke for 4 hours.

(4) Poach about 20 minutes in water up to 170°.

Mortadella **Mortadelle**

4 lb.	Lean pork meat
1 lb.	Pork fat
5 oz.	Potato Starch
	soft brine
	Beef medium of large hog casings
	Red food colouring
	Stock
Seasoning	(per lb.)
¼ oz.	Salt
1/10 oz.	Ground pepper
2/5 oz.	Whole pepper
2/10 oz.	Red colour
1/10 oz.	Cane sugar
1/10 oz.	Ground nutmeg
½ pt.	Red wine
1 pinch	curing salt

Method

(1) Cut fat into small dices; springkle some salt on it.

(2) Cut ceat in 1″ cube; place in soft brine 2 hours.

(3) Rinse, strain meat; grind finely.

(4) Place meat, fat, and seasoning (etc. wine) in mixer, beat slowly 3 minutes, adding 5 oz. potato flour while mixing.

(5) Add wine.

(6) Use a stuffing machine to fill casings.

(7) Place the sausages in a cool place for 58 hours.

(8) Smoke moderately for 6 hours, cook one hour very slowly in stock, cool in same for 2 hours.

(9) Remove from stock when cold; dry and store in refrigerator.

White Sausage **Budding Blanc**

5 qt.	Milk
3 lb	White bread, trimmed
3 lb	Fatback
2 lb	Lean pork meat
25 Eggs,	beaten
	Salt, pepper
1 pt.	Port wine
1	Jigger brandy
	Pork casing

Method

(1) Dice bread.

(2) Dice pork and fatback.

(3) Bring milk to a boil, pour over bread.

(4) Combine all ingredients (exc. casing); mix thoroughly and grind finely.

(5) Fill casings and twist to desired size.

(6) Drop sausages into boiling water, lowering heat immediately to prevent bursting. Use a ladle (or

small pot) to keep the water constantly in motion while simmering (about 20 minutes).

(7) To test for doneness, pierce one sausage, using a needle or sharp skewer. If the sausage rises to the surface, it is ready.

(8) Remove from water and place on sheet pans, cover with a cloth.

These sausages are best eaten the day they are made.

Dry Salami **Saucisson de Menage**

Soft brine

Garlic cloves

2 lb.	Lean pork meat
5 oz	Lean beef meat
8 oz	Fatback
1+ oz	Potato starch (dissolved in a little water)
	Pork casings

Seasoning

¼ oz	Salt per lb. Meat
1 pinch	Curing salt
1 pinch	Ground pepper
2 drops	Red colouring
1 pinch	4 Epice

Method

(1) Cut lean pork and beef in 1″ cubes, soak in soft brine 3 hours. Strain.

(2) Grind meat finely; grind fat with a slightly larger knife.

(3) Rub interior or mixer with garlic; place meat and remaining ingredients within and mix slowly for about one minute, adding fatback at end.

(4) Fill casings; tie. Soak in brine for about six hours.

(5) Place in drying room at a constant 60° temperature, until dried to desired consistency at which time they will be ready to be served (will take about 60 to 80 days to dry up).

Boiled Ham **Jambon Blanc**

1 Fresh ham, as lean as possible

3 gallons Brine

3 gallons Unsalted bouillon

Method

(1) Separete the ham from the shank, putting the shank away for another recipe.

(2) Bone the ham carefully by slidingthe bone out and lift the skin almost entirely in one piece using a very sharp knife. Trim most of the fat.

(3) Inject with special needle in all parts of the ham and soak the ham for 3 to 4 hours in the brine.

(4) Rinse the ham in clear water, roll in an appropriate size piece of cheesecloth, tie both ends, then the whole ham starting from one end to the other, as to make a perfect cylinder, but not too tight.

(5) Place ham in deep pan, cover with stock, bring to a boil and simmer at 150° for about 4 hours or 20 minutes per lb. Of meat.

(6) Remove from fire, unwrap, and wrap again, tightening up the strings. Place ham back in stock and cool off completely before unwrapping and slicing.

Flat Sausages **Crepinettes**

Method

(1) Make 2½ to 3 oz balls of sausage meat.

(2) Wrap in pre-washed and squeezed pork caul, do not wrap tightly.

(3) Shape into rectangular form; refrigerate until needed.

(4) Fry on both sides.

This item goes well with fresh mashed potatoes.

Larded Roast Pork in Aspic **Rôti de Porc Piqué**

4 lb. piece	Ham (centre cut if possible)
15	Lardons (strips of fatback, the lenght of the roast)
2 gallons	Good veal stock
	Sugar

Method

(1) Bone and skin meat.

(2) Using a special needle (Gardoir), clout the meat regularly with lardons.

(3) Tie up the roast with butcher's twine in regular spaces of ½".

(4) Sprinkle the meat with a little sugar (icing) and brown on all faces in a frying pan or a very hot oven.

(5) Put the meat in a deep covered pot, cover meat with veal stock and simmer slowly for about 30 minutes per lb., until tender.

(6) Place meat in deep service bowl.

(7) Cover with an aspic made with the cooking stock, cool off overnight and slice directly from the bowl.

8

FORCEMEATS, MARINADES AND GARNISHES

FORCEMEATS

Defination

Forcemeats are the combination of meat or fish and fat which is grounded and seasoned. There are three elements of forcemeat i.e.:

1. Fat
2. Meat
3. Seasoning

FAT

This is the most important element because it provides flavour and binding. Different types of fat used are Suet, Lard, Tallow or Dripping Mostly pork fat is used.

MEAT

Lean meats or scraps of meat can be used.

Seasoning

Traditional seasoning of forcemeat is Pate spice which consists of the following ingredients:

Pate Spice (As given by Master Chef August Escoffer)

Bayleaf	:	45 g
Ginger powder	:	20 g

Thyme	:	20 g
Mace	:	20 g
Coriander seeds	:	20 g
Black Peeper	:	45 g
Cinnamon	:	30 g
Cayenne Pepper	:	10 g
Nutmeg (grated)	:	40 g
White Pepper	:	45 g
Cloves	:	30 g

Sometimes Breadcrumbs or Panda or Blood is used as Binding.

In order to improve the appearance of forcemeat various garnishes may be used to provide colour contrast, texture contrast or use particular ingredients as identity of the dish.

Forcemeat Proportions

The percentage of meat to fat is regulated while preparing forcemeat. The proportion are as follows:

40% Dominant meat

30% Pork fat

30% Pork meat (lean)

These forcemeat forms the foundations of popular dishes for example galatines, pates, terrines, sausages and ballontines etc. Example of first forcemeat (La Farce de de Poisson) are given below:

Fist Forcemeat **La Farce de Poisson**

½kg	Pike and salmon or Rohu.
500 g	Shrimp or Scallops
60 g	fresh bread crumbs
2 N	Egg whites

To taste	Tabasco, Worcestershire Sauce.
2 cups	Heavy cream.

Pork Sunsagemeat **La force deporc anglaise.**

250 g	lean pork
150	ml in cold water
100 g	pork fat
15 g	seasoning
100 g	white breadcrumb

One can prepare beef sansagemeat or veal sansagemeat by replacing lean pork with beef or veal respectively.

HAMBURGERS

350 g	mixed beef
15 g	Salt
100 g	mixed pork fat
10 g	White pepper
100 g	white bread crumbs
1	pinch of allspice
100 g	cooked chopped onions
1 No	egg

Cromesquis

350 g	mixed cooked chicken meat
200 ml	chicken veloute
2	yolk of eggs
1	Pig caul.

Seasoning to taste.

MARINADES **CURES AND BRINES**

Definition

Marinades can be defined as a mixture of ingredients used to flavour, tenderize and to preserve the food items

There are two types of marinades:

(1) Cooked

(2) uncooked

Four possible combinations of ingredients may be used to prepare marinades they are:

(1) oil and acid

(2) oil spices/herbs

(3) acid and spices

(4) Salt and water

Cures and Brines are slightly different from marinades because their purpose is to preserve the food items. Their basic ingredients are salt as the base, sugar, sodium nitrate or Potassium nitrate (*suhaga*) and also little ascorbates and phosphates.

The purpose of using these ingredients is as follow:

(1) **Salt**—mainly used as a preservative because it causes dehydration by osmosis. But too much of salt has negative effect harsh taste, dry texture and spoiled colour.

(2) **Sugar**—It lessens the action of salt by retaining some of the moisture in product.

(3) **Nitrates**—This improves the colour in the product, also retards rancidity and prevent harmful bacteria like Clostridium botulism.

(4) **Ascorbates**—By adding ascorbates curing time in reduced.

(5) **Phosphates**—This helps in increasing the water binding capacity of the product during curing.

Method of Curing

The curing of meats is either done as dry curing that is by the use of salt cures or dry sugarcane cure. Or by Soaking in brine or by pumping brine in the meat.

Generally the salt cured or brine cured products are further preserved by smoking method.

SMOKED FOOD PRODUCTS

The purpose of smoking is to preserve the food products. Special wood chips or dust is used for this purpose. The items can be smoked either by hot smokes method i.e. at 130°F to 225°F or by cold smoke method at 72-100°F.

Method of Smoking

1. The product is to be fabricated for example trussing of chicken or fish or rounding of ham.
2. **CURING**—As described earlier the products can either be dry cured or soaked in brine or injected with brine.
3. **RINSING**—Wash and scrub with hot water and pat dry.
4. **PELLICLE FORMATION**—Hang in cooler to dry (in a refrigerator) till skin formation results this is caused by drying. It will take 6 hours to 24 hrs depending on the size of the product.
5. **SMOKING**—Smoke as desired by either hot smoke or cold smoke.

Example of smoked and cured products

(1) Bacon—Belly Portion—cured, smoked and partially cooked.

(2) Bacon—Loin Portion—cured smoked and cooked.

(3) Ham—scraps cured, cooked.

(4) Country Ham—dry cured one month or more

(5) Westphalian Ham—rubbed with salt and cured for two weeks then placed into a pickle for another two weeks, aged one month, soaked for hours and smoked with juniper twigs over wood fire for one week.

(6) Beef—Covered beef, Pastrami and dried beef (knuckle) poultry, veal and lamb are also smoked

Example of cures

(1) Special Dry Cure for Fish

1 kg	salt
½ kg	Brown sugar
2 tbsp	salt peter (suhaga)
2 tbsp	garlic powder
2 tbsp	onion powder
1 tbsp	crushed bayleaf
2 tbsp	ground all spice
2 tbsp	ground mace
1 tbsp	ground cloves

(2) gravad Lax Cure

1¼ kg	salt
3 kg	sugar
1 tbsp	crushed white pepper corns
2 tbsp	crushed dried jumper berries.

MUSTARD PICKLES (FOR VEGETABLES)

3 cups	white vinegar
60 g	Dijon mustard
1½ cup	Grain sugar
1tsp	Turmeric powder
1tsp	Ground cloves

PICKLED FRUIT

4 cups	Sugar
1 cup	Lider vinegar
1 cup	Water

4 No	Chinaman sticks
12 No	cloves

Boil to syrup consistency

ALAGRECQUE

1 cup	Water
1	clove of garlic
1 cup	Olive oil
4tsp	thyme
3 No	Lemon (juice)
1 No	Bay leaf
1 tbsp	White Vinegar
3/4 tsp	Coriander powder
1 stalk	Celery chopped
8 No.	Peppercorns
1 Stalk	Fennel chopped
¼ tsp	Salt

Boil to the contents whip in oil and use as required

BEER MARINADE (FOR MEATS)

750 ml	Ale or Dark beer
125 ml	White vinegar
7 tbsp	Sugar
1 No.	Onion sliced (medium size)
2 No	Bayleaves
5 No	cloves
1/3 tsp	Grounded black pepper
500 g	Crushed juniper berries.
1/3 tsp	All spice powder.

Marination time—1 week

WINE MARINATE (FOR MEATS)

1 litre	Red wine
150 ml	Vinegar
7tbsp	Oil
2tbsp	Salt
1	Onion (medium-sized sliced)
1 tsp	sugar
1 tsp	Thyme
1	Ginger fresh (small piece)
1 No.	Bayleaf
2 No.	Cloves
10 No.	Pepper corns

SOME INDIAN PICKLES

Mango Pickle (Yield 1 kg)

Green mango (Preferably *Gola aam*)	1kg
Red chillies	50 g
Kalongi (Onion seeds)	25 g
Salt	200 g
Saunf (Ani seed)	50 g
Methi (Fenu greek)	50 g
Haldi, (Turmeric in powder)	25 g
Mustard oil	500 ml.

Wash, clean destone and cut the mangoes into 8 pieces. Keep it for drying under the sun. In a clean bowl add all the *masalas*. Add ½ the oil and mix nicely. Add mango pieces and mix well with *masala*. Rub the masala into the mango pieces. Put the contents into a porcelain jar or glass jar and press nicely. Cover it and tied it with a cloth and keep for days. Mix thoroughly and add rest of the oil and the keep for eight days.

Mango Chutney

Green large grated mangoes	1 kg
Sugar	½ kg
Kali mirch (Peppercorns)	10 g
Big cardamom	10 g
Cinnamon	05 g
Bayleaf	1 No
Cumin seeds	1tsp
Salt	100 g
Vinegar	½ cup.

Peel and wash mango and grate them. Prepare sugar syrup of one thread consistency Grind the masala and add along with mangoes in the syrup cook for two minutes. Add vinegar. Cool the contents. Place it is a glass jar. Tie with a cloth and keep for three days. Variations can be made by adding sultana or melon seeds or dried dates are grated cocoanut in the syrup.

Sweet Mango Pickle

Jaggery	750 g
Green mango (*Gola aam*)	1 kg
Fenugreek (methi)	15 g
Aniseed (*saunf*)	25 g
Red chillies	25 g
Turmeric (Haldi powder)	25 g
Salt	100 g
Vinegar	½ g

Peel, wash and cut the mango into thin pieces. Prepare jaggery syrup with ½ cup of water. Grind the masala and add to the syrup. Add mango pieces and boil for two minutes the add vinegar. Cool and fill into a glass jar. Tie with a cloth and use after 8 days.

Mango Murraba

Green mango pulp into small pieces	1 kg
Sugar	750 g

Kewra essence and small cardamom to flavour. Prick mango pieces. Prepare the flavoured sugar syrup of one thread consistency. Add mango pieces. Put it in a tight fitting glass jar. Use it after two days.

Carrot Murraba

Carrot	1kg
Sugar	750 g

Peel wash and remove yellow core of carrots and cut it into small pieces. Soak it in lime water for one day. Take it out and dry. Prepare 2 thread consistency sugar syrup. Add the carrots and simmer for a few minutes. Cool and keep in a glass jar.

Mango pickle with black gram and Bitter gourd

Green Mango (gola aam)	1 kg
Whole red chilly	100 g
Bitter gourd (*karela*)	250 g
Bengal gram	½cup
Saunf (Aniseed)	50 g
Methi (Fenu greek)	50 g
Salt	250 g
Haldi (Turmeric)	50 g
Kalongi (onion seed)	50 g
Mustard oil	750 g

Clean, wash and cut the mangoes into eight pieces and dry under the sun. Peel wash and cover the karela with salt and sundry wash and dry on a cloth.

In a clean dry glass jar add pieces of mangoes, karela, Bengal gram (picked and washed, red chillies and masala then add ½ oil. Tie with a cloth and keep for three days. Mix well add rest of the oil and keep for ten days.

Lemon Pickle

Kagji lemon	1kg
Garam masala Powder	200 g
Salt	750 g
Ajwain	10 g

Soak the lemons overnight. Next morning dry under the sun. Cut the lemons into four segments without separation. Mix all the masala then stuff into each lemon. Place the lemons into a glass jar with right side up. Add masala and lemon juice. Cover, tie with a cloth and keep for seven days. Mix it very well and use it after 10th day.

CONJEE

This is a fermented, flavoured vegetable base refreshing drink. The Indians mostly prepare it in the months of February, March and April. This can be served as an appetizer before the meals.

Gajar ki Canjee

Black carrots	250 g
Black rye	50 g
Salt	200 g
Water	1.5 litres
Red chilly powder	2tsp

Use a earthenware pot or a glass jar. Clean, wash and dry the pot. To add flavour to the canjee, take a live charcoal piece, sprinkle cumin seeds, asafoetida (*hing*) powder along with little *asli* (pure) ghee and cover the pot or jar to be used for conjee preparation. The scented smoke will nicely settle in the vessel. Grind rye into a fine powder. Mix chilly powder. Peel wash and cut the carrots into small piece. In a separate pan add water, carrots, rye powder, mirch powder mix well and pour into the prepared vessel. Tie with a cloth and keep for three days in the sun or till the rye particles become white in colour.

Loki Conjee

Parboil the loki, rest is as above. This conjee gets ready in one day.

Beetroot conjee

Cook the beetroot pieces and proceed as above.

GARNISHING

This comes as one of the responsibilities of chef gar-de-manger. His department has to supply the material of garnishing for the various dishes prepared at the other stations in the kitchen. The chef gar-de-manger has to carefully study the menu of each outlet and plan the requirement of raw material for the garnish of various items well in advance to maintain good relations with other departments.

Some example of the material required course-wise may be as follow:

For soups or Potages

(1) Clarification material

(2) Chicken quennells

(3) Pork quennells

(4) Veal quennells

(5) Game quennells

(6) Sliced bone marrows

(7) cooked prawns shrimps etc.

(8) Collection of various fresh vegetable cuts like, juliennes, macidoine, dices, Batonnets, paysanne. Oblique, olivette, mirepoix and matignons.

(9) Fillings for bouches

(10) Brunoise of chicken and Ham.

FISH COURSE

Fish quennls slices and dices of lobsters, cray fishmeats, stoned olives and grapes. Fish eggs, slices or dices of truffles; oysters etc.

ENTRES

juliennes of ham,

tongue

juliennes of truffles,

tomato,

celery.

Salpicons, fillings for vol-an-vent, large pastry cases, stoned olives, chicken livers, Dices of pork fat, lardons, Barding pork fat, Sheets, Dices of vegetables, Chicken, Ham, meats, bone marrow slices.

Main Courses

Various compound butter, various cold sauces, water, asparagus tips, Grated egg yolks, Choppol egg white. Cuts of various vegetables, Diced Ham, meats and chicken.

Sweet Course

Sausage meat, Diced meat, salpicons, Anchovy, sardines (Puffpastry fillings) forcemeat of meat, poultry and game (Pie), vegetables and meats for Ravioli filling cut vegetables and meats, Ham and chicken for Pizzas.

Classical Garnishes

(1) **Alexandra**: This is in the honour of the King of Britain and Ireland in 1844. Truffles sliced, artichoke bottoms, shredded chicken.

(2) **Allemande**: In the style of German cooking Sauerkraut, pickled salt pork or smoked sausage.

(3) **Alsacienne:** In the style of Alsac cooking now in France.

(4) **Sauerkraut** and Cabbage.

(4) **Americaine:**—In the style of American cooking Slices of lobster tail and truffles.

(5) **Dieppoise:**—Shrimps, mussels and mushroom.

(6) **Milanaise and Juliennes** of ham, tongue, truffles and tomatoes.

(7) **Regence** (i) For fish—fish quennells, crayfish tails, mushrooms, oysters, fish eggs, sliced truffles.

(8) **Reform**—Juliemnes of Ham, tongue, beetroot, white of egg, gherkins

(9) **Viennoise**—slices of lemon, anchovy, sieved egg yolks and chopped egg white, parsley.

(10) **Zingara:**—Juliennee of Ham, mushroom, tongue and truffles.

9

COLD BUFFET LAYOUT AND PREPARATIONS

In the modern day catering systems most of the hotels have cold food display along with hot food dishes. This has become a permanent feature specially at Lunchtimes.

Taking into consideration the customer's perception the following factors affect the buffet quality

a. **Function room:**—It may be the speciality restaurant or a banquet hall or a coffee shop, its size, height of ceiling, interior decor, lighting are to be taken into consideration.

b. **Hardware:**—These are silver platters, mirror, copper pans, stainless chafers, turreens, crystalware, tablecloth, sativ and skirting all contribute to the quality.

c. **Decorative pieces or "Piece Monte":**—This will include flower arrangements, sculpture make out of ice, tallow, butter and salt dough.

d. **Food Displayed:**

(1) **Arrangement**—This will be mainly responsible for customers initial overall impression of the food. Remember "one never gets the second chance to make the first impression".

(2) **Workmanship**—Most of the guests will appreciate the workmanship in displayed tools but the

important aspect in the quality control point which evaluate the integrity of workmanship and plays an important role in controlling quality perceptions.

A chef focus will be in the area of food arrangement and workmanship.

Chef's de Froid, is one of the assistants of chef garde-manger, responsible for the preparation, dressing and the serving of cold buffets. To carry out these duties he or she should be familiar with the work concerned with larder preparations. These include preparation of aspics, chaud-froid sauces, pies, galantines, terrines, patis, mousses or cold souffles, prawns etc. as well as the various fillings for sandwiches and cold savouries, canapes etc. He should also be skilled in the cooking and dressing of fish, shellfish, hams, tongue and other pickled products. In addition to these duties, the chef must have an artistic flair with experience in the preparation and use of Aspic which will help him in decorating and garnishing of cold food dishes. He or she should be able of carve ice, fats and also should be skilled in the use of carving knives without handling the cold food with his finger.

The foods which can be served on a cold buffet includes:—

a. *Forcemeat preparations:*—Galantines, terrines, pâtes, mousses, ballontines, and pies.

b. Plain or stuffed and poached fish like salmon, trout, rohu, zingara, or crayfish, crawfish, lobsters salads, or mayonnaised fish or shell fish or dressed crabs.

c. Roast meats, poultry and game like roast beef or ribs of lamb or mutton or roast leg of veal, Bestend of veal, lamb or mutton, or roast pork whole or in cut or roast suckling pig, or roast duck, chicken, quail or a goose etc. or a crow roast.

d. Smoked meats and fish like smoked salmon, cod or rohu or smoked and dressed Ham, on tongue or brawn. Pickled ox-tongue or corned beef.

e. Classical appetizers like *Pate de foi gras, caviar,* Plover's eggs and smoked salmon etc.

f. All kinds of cold salad preparations like vegetable-based, fruit-based, fish based and meat and poultry-based salads.

g. Sandwiches like Smörgasbord, canapes, zakuskis etc.

h. appetizers and cold soups like melon, cocktails, stuffed eggs, fruit cocktail, grape fruit, sea food cocktail etc. Jellied consommes gazpacho etc.

i. Cheese board with hard, semi-hard soft and blueveined cheese, fruit basket, and cold sweets, and an assorted bread dispaly from bakery department when preparing for a cold buffet layout, plan the pattern and design well in advance and if possible draw it on a piece of paper. The display of food is generally done on tables which may be in rectangular, square, round or an oblong shape. The table can be tiered with wooden blocks or Emply soft drink crates and then covered with dark colour satins.

Appectizers, salads, cold sauces, cold soups and breads, should be displayed on the lower tiers while entries and main dishes along with accompaniments should occupy the middle areas. The centre piece or piecemonte should be displayed prominiently at the top centre of the table. The display of fresh fruits and cold sweets and breads should be done on separate tables. Glassware crockery and cutlery should be displayed on adjoining tables.

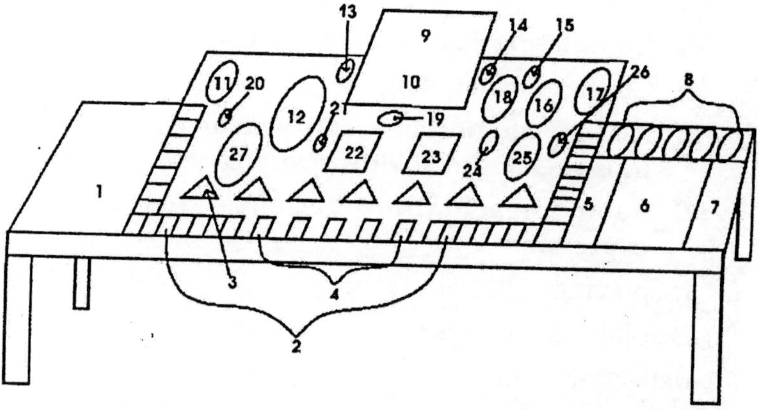

1 Glassware, Crockery, Cutllery
2 Salads
3 Cold Sauces
4 Appetizers
5 Breads & Butter
7 Cheese Board
7 Fruit Basket
8 Cold Sweets
9 Piece monte
10 Caviar on Ice.
11 Smoked Ham
12 Cold Lobster
13 Timbale
14 Cucumber Basket
15 Stuffed Eggs.
16 Galantine
17 Crown Roast
18 Roast Leg of Lamb
19 Cold Beef
20 Mayonnaise
21 Pickled Veg.
22 Canape
23 Platte Mirror
24 Compound Butters
25 Duck A L'orange
26 Red Pepper Mouse
27 Mayonnaise Rohu

Fig. 9.1

PRINCIPLES OF PRESENTATION, RELATIONSHIP TO ART

Food and Aesthetics—When it is pleasing, food nourishes the spirit as well as the body.

(1) **Food presentation becomes a sensual art form when you create an ambiance by:**

(a) Arranging food in orderly and pleasing groupings on a plate or platter.

(b) Combining colour, texture and flavour.

(c) Choosing certain plates or other serviceware.

(d) Considering table appointments.

(e) Considering lighting.

(f) Alerting the instincts and whetting the appetite, thus creating a multi-sensory chain reaction.

(2) Food presentation becomes a vehicle of expression by:

(a) Displaying cultural styles.

(b) Displaying life styles.

(c) Reflecting traditions.

(d) Showing care or lack of care.

(3) Combining food and aesthetics is based on pleasure since food has the ability to gratify most of our senses.

(a) **Aroma**—the first stimulus we perceive at mealtime and one of the more lasting sensations after dinner.

(b) **Taste**—the most personal of all the senses. What one person like, another may dislike.

(c) **Touch**—texture involves the way food feels in our mouths. A variety of textures makes an interesting melange in the mouth.

(d) **Visual**—Visual impact of food presentation is usually dependent on colour. Colourful food is festive and appealing.

Basic Fundamentals and Principles

The same basics are applied regardless of which art or craft you are considering. The same design rules are followed for architecture, painting, sculpture, dance, landscaping and food presentation.

(1) Fundamentals of Art

(a) Colour—The most exciting ingredient for visual impact is based on principles of colour harmony:

(1) **Simultaneous contrast**—colours standing opposite one another in the colour wheel lend brilliance and purity to one another; red-green, purple-yellow, orange-blue.

(2) **Analogous combination**—colours next to one another on the circle create a subtle effect; orange-yellow, blue-green, purple red.

(3) **Monochromatic combinations**—selecting tones and values of the same colour.

(b) Line/Form—line and form go hand-in-hand. Line is the skeleton, mass is the flesh. Line gives the impression, mass provides the form.

(1) Line associations—most people have come to associate certain lines with definite qualities:

(a) Straight lines suggest stability, dignity, strenght.

(b) Curved lines suggest grace, beauty, movement.

(c) Weak lines lack direction and credibility and suggest decay.

(2) Border patterns—line also represents the path that the eye follows:

(a) One requirement of the border pattern is that is should be repetitive.

(b) Border design should first be composed of one or more design units (but less than five units) used exclusively around the border.

(3) Form—developed from line to produce a fuller meaning to a design.

(a) Shape or form, because it is based on a line, carries with it associations with definite quatties.

(b) Exploit natural shapes of form wherever possible. Some forms have visually appealing shapes and can be used to give interest to forms that are not themselves very attractive.

(c) Add variety and "surprise" by introducing new cuts, tools and molds.

(c) **Texture**—adds appeal to food when used to develop contrast.

(1) Assure proper texture.

(2) Utilize natural texture variety.

(3) Modify through different preparations.

(2) Principles of Design

(a) Balance—The optical coordination of mass and colour (visual weight).

(1) Formal balance—equal areas of mass (visual) are placed on either side oa central axis.

(a) size

(b) colour

(c) texture

(d) distance from centre.

(2) Counter balance—When an inceptive axis runs across (diagonally) the area.

(3) Informal balance—When units of mass may differ in size on each side of the axis, but when viewed together in the completed design, produce equal optical balance (equal visual weight).

(b) Proportion—The size relationship of one part of the presentation to another, dealing with the presentation as a whole rather than the individual items within.

(c) Rhythm—In design, obtained when the flow of movement has definite harmonious arrangement:

(1) Optical rhythm should exist between lines, forms, and colours.

(2) The structure of the design must have coordination to be appealing and effective.

(d) Unity—A sense of togetherness assuring that all parts work together to accomplish the same end. . . And arrangement or presentation that correctly applies the required qualities of rhythm, proporation and balance.

(1) All parts of the presentation should fit together in such a way that there is no discord or conflict among them—no competition.

(2) The design must also complement the form.

(e) Focal Point—The point of emphasis. This is the area that has the bulk of the weight and supports the rest of the presentation. The focal point is supported by:

(1) Proper proportion.

(2) Colour.

(3) Texture.

(4) Line.

FOODS BY COLOUR

Red colour

Apple	Currant	Raspberries
Blood orange	Pink Grapefruit	Strawberries
Boso Pear	Cranberries	Tomatoes
Cherry	Pomegranate	Watermelon
Plums	Rhubarb	Beet
Italian Onion	Radish	Red lentils
Red leaf lettuce	Red pepper	Caviar
Crabs	Lobster	Red snapper
Salmon		
Red-rind cheese: Gouda, Edam, Fontina	Shrimp	Lumpfish caviar

Orange

Apricoat	Cantaloupe	Clementine
Crenshaw melon	Kumquat	Mango
Nectarine	Organe	Papaya
Peach	Persian melon	Persimmon
Pumpkin	Tangerine	Acorn squash
Sweet potatoes	Chilli peppers	Cheddar cheese
Yams	Bell peppers	

Yellow

Apple	Banana	Bartlett pear
Comice pear	Grapefruit	Lemon
Mango	Pineapple	Corn
Turnips: Rutabaga	Wax beans	Yellow peppers
Yellow squash	Yellow tomato	Cheese
Golden caviar	Egg yolks	Butter

Brown/Beige

Mushrooms	Potatoes (unpeeled)	Dates
Figs (dried)	Raisins	Almonds
Walnuts	Pecans	Coconut
Seckel pear	Kiwi (unpeeled)	Barley
Wheat berries	Lentils	Fried onions
Meat	Chocolate	Croutons

(a) Black (Purple-black)

Olives	Truffles	Blackberries
Black currants	Elderberries	Prunes

Fig Grapes	Blueberry	Raisins
Caviar	Eggplant Mussels	Black beans

(b) Black (purple-scarlet)

Boysenberry	Plum	Grape
Cranberry	Fig	Beet
Cabbage	Red onion	

Green

Anjou pear	Fig	Apple
Gooseberries	Grapes	Greengage plums
Honeydew	Kiwi	Lime
Watermelon	Winter melon	Fennel stalks
Olive	Green pepper	Leeks
Peas	Snow peas	Spinach
Scallion	String beans	Celery
Zucchini	Asparagus	Broccoli
Artichoke	Brussels sprouts	Cabbage
Boke choy	Broad beans	Okra
Arugula	Dandelion greens	Cucumber peel
Greens for salads:	Gherkins	Watercress
Bibb lettuce, Romaine,		Sorrel
Boston, Iceberg, Escarole,		Pickles
Chicory, Kale,		
Chervil	Mint	Chives
Dill	Parsley	Basil

White (fruit interiors)

Apple (peeled)	Banana (peeled)	Casaba melon
Pears (peeled)	Grapefruit segments	Honeydew melon
White currants	Coconut (gravted)	Lichees
Bean shoots	Cauliflower	Celeriac
Bamboo shoots	Dried white bean	Endive
Onion	Parsnip	Potato
Mushrom (cultivated)	Water chestnut	White radish
Turnip	scallion bulbs	Cucumber (peeled)
Daikon (Japanese radish)		Hearts of palm
Great Northern benas	Lima Beans (dried)	Summer squash (peeled)
Zucchini (peeled)	Rice	Brazil nuts (shelled)
Cashews	Fennel bulb	Scallops
Fish fillets	Egg white	

GELATINE AND ASPIC GELES

Background

The commerical production of gelatine was started in A.D. 1890. Charles knox first developed gelatine in granular form. However in 17th century, after the French revolution it was made mandatory to offer gelatine as a nutrition supplement in soups and stews.

Production

Raw material, i.e. bones are given a series of dilute acid baths and then a soaking in lime water. Then collagen is made to dissolve in hot water concentrated and filtered and the cooled and dished. This is sold in the form of sheet or granules. Collagen is an insoluble fibrous protein in concetive tissue and in bones that fields gelatine on prolong heating with water. The bones used for production of gelatine are knuckles, hooves, feet and tail portions of cattles or veal.

Some helpful terms:—

1. Gelatine—Glutenous incomplete protein derived from collagen.
2. Gelee—An unclarified concentrated stock.
3. Aspic (gelee)— A clarified glutenous stock.
4. Aspic—A finished decorative mould of cooked food suspended in aspic gelee.

Role of Aspic gelee in food production

(1) To preserve moisture, so item will not dry and thereby preserving colour.

(2) To add flavour and nutritional value.

(3) Enhance the appearance.

Basically there are two types of aspic gelee (a) clear gelee and (b) Amber colour gelee from brown bones.

Preparation of Aspic gelee

Aspic gelee can be prepared in the kitchen by adding gelatine powder to stocks.

Basic recipe for Aspic gelee

3 kg	Mirepoix veal or mutton knuckles chopped.
3-4 No.	Mirepoix calves feet (boned and blanched).
250 g	Mirepoix fresh pork rind (blanched)

100 g Mirepoix onion

100 g Mirepoix carrots

2 pieces Mirepoix celery

2 No. Mirepoix leeks

25 g Mirepoix Bouquet garni

10 litre Mirepoix water

Blanch the bones and rind and refill with fresh water. Bring it to boil. Boiling liquid. Simmer for 5 to 6 hr on low heat. Add mirepoix and bouquet garni, Pour stock through a strainer cool, remove all grease. Reduce to 5 litres.

Clarification

1 kg minced (lean) meat (beef or mutton)

6 eggs white

500 gms mirepoix.

2-3 No lemon in juice

1½ cup of Maderia wine.

Allow the stock to cool overnight mix all the ingredients well and add cold stock. Bring it to boil stirring continuously with spatula. Simmer for 1 hour and strain through a cheese cloth or muslin cloth and use as required.

Variations

Amber colour gelee can be obtained by using browned bones and mirepoix in the stock. Similarly game aspic jelly can be prepared by using veal bones with game bones.

CHAUDFROID SAUCES

Chaud froid mean hot cold, i.e. sauces which are normally served warm and served cold. For the preparation of chaud froid the basic souces or there derivatives are mixed with aspic jelly and then cooled down.

White chaud froid sauce

Bechamel, veloute	500 ml
Aspic gelee	400 ml.
Cream fresh	500 ml.

Boil the veloute or Bechamel. Add aspic and reduce by 1/3rd. Add cream to required consistency. Strain through a strainer into a clean bowl. Stir to cool. From this white chaud froid sauce variations in colours can be achieved by adding the natural food colours. For example a pink chaud froid will be made by add fresh tomato puree or puree of red peppers or a green chaud froid can be prepared by adding puree or spinach or puree of fine herbs. Wines many be added to give extra flavour to the sauce.

Brown chaud froid

Use demi glace flavoured with tomatoes or garlic along with port or Sherry wine. For duck dishes use flavour of orange by adding orange juice and orange zest. For lamb or mutton dishes use mint flavour in demi-glace.

The chaud froid sauces can be made in advane and may be melted at the time of use.

Cold soups

Chilled strawberry soup with cantaloupe 4 servings

Fresh strawberries	500 g
Orange Juice	1 cup
Diluted cornflour	1tbsp
All spice powder	1/8 tsp
Cinamon	1/8 tsp
Lemon rind	1tsp
Grain sugar	½ cup
Lemon juice	1tbsp

Buttermilk	1cup
Cantaloup slices	120 g
Grand Marnier to taste	

Method

Remove strawberries 6 for garanish. Puree the remaining berries. Add orange juice. Add diluted cornflour, heat mixture stirring occasionally until the boil comes. Cook until thick. Remove from heat and put in a glass bowl. Add sugar lemon zest and juice. Then add buttermilk and chill for 8 hours. After 4th hour add thinly sliced cantaloupe and garnish of sliced strawberries. Before serving mix in Grand Marimier.

Gazpacho 8-10 servings

3 large	Tomatoes (fresh and ripe)
2 large	Cucumbers (fresh)
1 bunch Green	onions
1 medium size	capcicum
¼ cup	celery
1 clove	garlic
1 tbsp	vinegar
1 tbsp	Olive oil
¼ tbsp	Tobasco sauce.
½ tbsp	Thyme
½ tbsp	Basil
1 tbsp	Chopped parsly.
300 ml	Consomme

Peel and cut tomatoes into small dices. Peel and cut cucumber into small dices. Clean and cut green onion and green pepper small dices. Clean and cut celery stem into small dices. Make the paste of garlic. Combine all the ingredients. Allow to chill 12-24 Hours to achieve blending of flavours.

Variations can be given by using any of the following dash of bitters, dash of Worcestershire sauce, 1 tsp Red chilly powder, ½ tsp roasted cummin seed powder or ½ tsp of roasted corriander powder.

Geleed consomme:—Any good concentrated consomme white or brown can be served chilled in individual cups by mixing with aspic gelee.

Chicken salad **Salade de volaille**

1	Broiler .chicken (roasted or boiled)
2	hard boiled eggs
2	peeled tomatoes
4	gherkins or one little cucumber
2	slice of pineapples
50 g	finely chopped onions
1	crisp heart of lettuce
250 ml	vinaigrette

Method

Olive parsley or chill, for garinsh. Debone the chicken and slice the flesh thinly. Cut gherkins, 1 eggs, 1 tomato and pineapple into dices. Mix with chicken and marinate in dressing. Live a glass bowl with lettuce leaves and make a base of shreaded lettuce. Place the chicken and lettuce garnich with quarters of eggs and tomatoes, olives, a piece of pineapple alongwith parsley and dill leaves. Serve chilled.

Galantine de Poulet

2 Nos.	Chicken Broilers
250 g	fillet of veal

250 g	fillet of pork
500 g	fat Bacon
100 g	of lean ham
100 g	of cooked pickled tongue
100 g	of larding bacon
50 g	truffles or olives
25 g	pistachio nuts
40 g	of spiced salt
2 tbsp	Brandy
4	Eggs

Method

Singe, wipe and draw the chickens. Trim off the weights at Ist joint and legs at the joint with drumstick. Debone the chickens taking care not to damage the skin. Separate the flesh of chicken from the skin. Soak the skin in cold water. Dry well and spread out on clean cloth. Remove the flesh of second chicken and cut it into ¼ inch strips. Cut ham, tongue and bacon same size. Marinade them in brandy along with truffles, pistachio nuts for 1 hour. Make a forcemeat with rest of chicken flesh, veal, pork and bacon fat. Season with salt and bind with eggs. Spread a layer of forcemeat along the centre of chicken skin. Set a layer of marinated fillets neatly on top, sprinkle with truffles or olives and pristachio nuts reapeat till all the forcemeat and fillets have been used. Top with layer of forcemeat. Draw the skin carefully around the forcemeat and roll the galantine in a large sausage shape. Tie in a muslin cloth with both ends tightly secured. Now poach in a concentrated chicken stock. for 1½ hours. Drain carefully, cool slightly, unwrap the cloth, re-roll and tie tightly and let it cool when cold enough. Remove cloth decorated and cool with aspic gelee and serve sliced.

Boeuf en Gelee

Daub of Beef

1.5 litre	oil
½ litre	vinegar
Tabsp	mustard pd.
	sliced chieves
6 Nos	Pork knuckles
2 No	Shanks of veal
1 Piece	Smoked Baconrind
1.5 kg	Beef chuckrib
1 kg	ham
1 cup	white wine
½ cup	Tomato puree
15 ml	cider vinegar
60 g	Gelatin
For sachet	
8 Nos	Bayleaves
1 tbsp	Thyme
8	whole cloves
8 pieces	all spice
little parsly stems	
6	cloves of garlic
1 tbsp	Pepper corns
1 tbsp	Red pepper pd.
½ tsp	Cumin seed

Chicken stock to cover.

1 cup each of blanched and diced onion, turnip, carrot, capcium

Method

Combine meats, sachet, wine, puree, stock. Boil and simmer under cover for 3 hour or till meat is tender. Remove meat and cool. Cut meat is small dices strain liquid and reduce by one-third, add vinegar. Dissolve gelatine in warm stock and add to broth. Add vegetable garnish and meat dices season. Set in a loaftin.

Salmon Mousse

500 g	Cooked salmon flesh
1½ tbsp	Gelatin
½ cup	Fish stock
1 tsp	Salt
Dash of Worcestershire sauce	
1 tbsp	Chopped dill
½ cup	Sour cream
½ cup	Whipped cream
¼ cup	Dry white wine

Method

Prepare the puree of salmon. Soak gelatine in warm fish stook. Whip the cream. Clean he mould. Place the puree of fish + gelatine + seasoning + Worcestershire sauce + sour cream + chopped dill. Mix lightly when starts to thicken, add whipped cream and mix lightly. Chill till set.

Blue cheese and Ham mousse

4 tsp	Gelatine
½ cup	Chicken stork
120 g	Ham
90 g	Roquefort fort cheese.
2 cloves	Garlic sauted in butter
	Seasoning to taste

1 cup	Heavy cream
2	egg yolks

Method

Soak the gelatine in warm chicken stock. Cut dices of Ham. Softened the cheese add egg yolks and garlic sauted in butter. Mix all the ingredients lightly and fold in the cream. Chill in a prepared mould.

Tomato mouśse

500 g	Brunnoise of celery flavoured with Dill and sauted.
1 litre	Tomato juice
2 tbsp	sugar
½ tsp	salt
½ tsp	Tabasco
1 tsp	Worcestershire sauce
1¼ cup	Whipped cream

Method

Combine tomato juice with sugar, salt, Tobasco and Worcester Shire sauce. Soak gelatine in little warm water. Mix together tomato juice gelatin and celery. Then fold in the whipped cream slowly, Chill in a mould.

Three flavoured vegetable Pate en croute

1 kg	Chicken meat
½ kg	Pork fat
Seasoing to taste	
500 g	Spinach
3 cloves	Garlic
120 g	Tomato pures
1 tsp	fresh basil

120 g	cooked carrot
1 tsp	fresh terragon
750 g	Bread flour
85 g	Butter
1	egg
10 g	Salt
5 g	Baking powder
30 g	Milk powder

3¼ water to build the dough.

Method

Prepare the chicken forcemeat adding little ice cubes while grinding. Divide into three equal parts. Puree one part of forcemeat with pureed spinach and garlic. Puree second part of forcemeat with pureed tomato paste and basil. Puree third part of forcemeat with puree carrot and fresh terragon. Layer each forcemeat in dough lined loaf tin. Cover with dough. Bake in the oven in a bain-marie for 1 to 1¼ Hour. Cool under pressure.

Sandwiches

Sandwich may be hearty and substancial meal. They are made of one or more slices of bread, spread with one a more kinds of fillings. They may be closed or open placed like Zakuski, Canapés and Smorrebrod

Preparation Tips

(1) Use one day old bread. If very fresh bread to be used, chill for few hours. Different varieties of breads like white bread, brown, bread, rolls, pummer nickle, rye bread etc.

(2) Cut slices of ½ inch thickness.

(3) Cream fresh butter and mix other additives like mustard, garlic, parsley, lemon, celery essence, etc. for spreads.

(4) Always use fresh ingredients for filling which can be grated cheese, chutney, fresh vegetables like tomato, cucumber, spinach, letture etc., cooked cold meat, poultry, game, poached fish, seafood, ham, sausages, fresh fruit etc. Avoid having too much fillings or topping.

(5) Cut sandwiches in beautiful shapes and wrap in foil and damp cloth.

Types of Sandwiches

(1) Conventional sandwiches

These are made of white or brown sandwich bread with a choice of butter spread or fillings. It is garnished and cut into different fancy geometrical shapes.

(2) Tea Sandwiches

The bread is cut very thin. Butter spread, fillings and garnish are used. The sandwiches are cut into fingers or small triangles or squares with pastry cutters and used to give fancy shapes.

(3) Buffet and reception sandwiches

Thinly cut sandwich bread with butter spread, filling and garnish. Cut into fancy shape with pastry cutters garnish with parsly and watercress.

(4) French sandwiches

Prepared from french loaf with conventional and spread and fillings. It is garnished and cut into neat strips and served with parsley or watercress.

(5) Open sandwiches

Bread with conventional butter spreads and fill ings. It is serve on a plate, no garnish necessary, an open colourful presentation is sufficient. These are the national food of Scandinavian countries, i.e. Norway, Sweden, Denmark and Northern Germany.

(6) Canapés

Any base like salted biscuit, bread white or brown or puff pastry pieces can be used. Conventional butters, fillings and garnishes are to be used to make them very colourful.

Some fancy sandwiches

(1) Rainbow sandwich

Bread slices	4 Nos
Butter	30 g
Mint chutney	½ tsp
Cheese	10 g
Boiled egg	½ no
Mayonnaise	1 tsp
Chopped ham	10 g
Tomato sauce	½ tbsp

Method

Butter 2 slices of bread on one side each and the remaining two on both the sides. Mix grated cheese with chutney. Finely chop the hard boiled egg and mix with mayonnaise. Shred hams and mix with tomato sauce. Take a slice of bread with one side buttered and apply mint filling on it. Cover with a bread buttered on both the sides. Apply egg filling on the second slice and cover with a slice buttered on both the sides. Apply the ham filling and cover with remaining slice of bread. Press lightly all the slices together. Trim and cut into strips and serve.

2. Pinwheel sandwich

Fresh bread	1 slice cut lengthwise
	1 hard boiled egg
	10 g butter
	¼ sp chilli sauce

Salt to taste

Pepper Powder a Pinch

Mustard powder a pinch

Take the slice of bread and remove the crust. Soften the bread. Mash the hard boiled egg add butter, seasoing and blendwell. Spread the filling evenly on bread and roll it. Wrap it and leave for 10 minutes. Cut the roll into 1" thick slices.

3. Ribbon Sandwiches

Brown bread	2 slices
White bread	2 slices
Butter 30 gms	
Cheese	15 gms
Pineapple	½ ring
Seasoning to taste	
Mustard powder	a pinch
Tomato (firm)	1 small.
Cheese	10 g
Mint—a few springs	
Corriander leaves—	

a few fresh coconut grated—5gms peanut—5gms

Method

Butter one slice each of brown bread and white bread on one side and the remaining two on both sides. Make pineapple cheese filling, tomato cheese filling and mint filling as given in previous recipes. Take a slice of white bread with one side buttered and spread pineapple cheese filling on it. Cover with brown bread buttered on both the sides. Apply tomato cheese filling on the second slice and cover with white bread slice buttered on both the sides. Apply chutney and peanut filling on it and cover with the remaining slice of brown bread. Press lightly all the slices together. Wrap and chill. Then trim and cut into thin ribbons.

4. Checker Board Sandwiches

Cream 30 g whipped.

Cheese 30 g

Mustard powder ¼ tsp

Butter 40 g

Black pepper powder 1/4 tsp

Brown bread 2 slices

White bread 2 slices

Method

Grate cheese, mix with cream and season. Prepare a stack like in ribbon sandwiches using half the butter and filling. Chill and cut into ½ slices. Now alternate the strips so that white strip in directly above a dark strip making a stack of 4 slices, spreading with butter and the filling between the slices as before. Keep under weight for sometime in a refrigerator and cut into ½" checkerboard.

APPENDIX I

TERMINOLOGY OF GAR DE MANGER

Garde Manger	Cold kitchen
Buffet	Table to arrange food
Buffet Froid	Cold Buffet
Buffet Zone	An individual buffed of equal foods and set-up designed to have large amount of covers served as fast as possible
A la carte	Your choice of menu
Hors d'Œuvre	A small attractive and tasty titbit.
Anipasto	Italian appetizer; variety of meat, fish and vegetable
Zakuski	Russian hous d' œuvre made from toast and various topings and covered with aspic (larger than canapes.)
Canape	Tiny open faced sandwich
Bouquet Garni	Carrot, celery, onion pique, leeks tied together
Piece Montee	Large, main centerpiece of whole buffet
Grosse piece	Centerpiece of individual food tray
Brace of Pheasant	One female and one male pheasant
Bellevue	Beautiful view
Homard en Bellevue	Lobster
Chemiser	To coat (Chaud Froid)

Bain Marie	Water bath or ice holder
Piquer	To insert (example: onion piquer)
Socle	Base of any material used to raise a food item
Sc. Verte	Green Herb Sauce
Vinaigrette	Vinegar, oil, herbs and spices
Farcir	To stuff
Farci	Stuffed
Farce Forcemeat	Various seasoned ground foods
Gratin Forcemeat	Cooked forcemeat which is usually added to a raw forcemeat
Galantine	A forcemeat wrapped in its own skin
Ballontine	Aforcemeat stuffed in a leg and shaped like a ballot and braised and mostly served hot
Terrine	Earthenware mold (round or oval)
Panada	Binding agent made of flour bread or other starch products
Mousse	A mixture of cooked ingredients pureed and held together with unflavoured gelatin, veloute sauce and aspic gelee mixed with cream and flavored with wine
Quenelle	Dumplings
Aspic Gelee	A stock with gelatine added and clarified
Chaud-Friod	Hot- Cold

Sauce Chaud– Froid	Bechamel or veloute with gelatin and heavy cream
Fumet	Essence of fish
Court Bouillon	Pre preparation of a stock (mostly fish)
Brillant Savarin	Statesman, writer or gourmet
Medaillion	Round slice of meat
Noisette	Small steak
Tranche	1" to 2" slice
Fume	Smoked
Saumon Fume	Smoked Salmon
La Truite Fume	Smoked Trout
Fumer	Smoking
Poche	Poaching
Bard	To surround meat products with the slice of fat
Al Dente	Firm to the bite

PATE TERMS

Pate	Seasoned forcemeat or ground meats or dough
Pate en croute	Meat pie or seasoned forcemeatin crust
Pate Maison	House pate or style of the house
Pate Facon du Chef	Style of the Chef
Pate de Foie Gras	Must have 75% goose liver
Pate de Foie	Pate of liver
Foie Gras	Fat liver of the goose
Oie	Goose

GAR DE MANGER EQUIPMENT

Timbale and Dariole	A small mold
Hatelet	Decorative silver skewer
Spring of hinge mold	Collapsible type mold used for production of Pate en croute
Barquette	Boat shaped molds
Poissoniere	An oblong fish poaching pan
Ravier	An oval or round appetiser dish

CAVIAR TERMS

Beluga	Largest variety of sturgeon family
Osetra	Middle variety of sturgeon family
Malosol	Means little salt
Sol	Salty
Blinis	A dollar size buckwheat pancake
Ikra	Russian Beluga Caviar

MUSHROOM TERMS

Champignon	White button mushroom (domestically grown)
Cepes	Stone mushroom
Chantrelles or Girolles	Yellow mushroom
Morrel (English)	Sponge mushroom
Morrilles (French)	Sponge mushroom
Truffle	Fungus fruit that matures underground

LOBSTER TERMS

Coral	Unborn eggs of a female lobster
Thomalli	liver of the lobster
Mother	Stomach of the lobster

APPENDIX-II

LIST OF SPICES, HERBS AND SEASONINGS

	Name	Description and Source	Uses
1.	Allspice	Dried Berry of pimento (not pimiento) tree, grown in West Indies. Flavour resembles blend of cinnamon, nutmeg and cloves, hence the name.	Used whole in pickling, soups preserved fruit, boiling fish, spiced meat and gravy. Ground allspice are used to season pot roasts, basked goods apple butter, conserves, ketchup, minced meat.
2.	Anise	Dried seed of plant belonging to celery family. Imported from Spain, Netherlands, Mexico	Sprinkled on coffee cake, sweet rolled cookies; in sweet pickles; flavouring cough syrups. Licorice product, candies in chocolate cake icing, in anisette liqueur.
3.	Apple Pie Spice	Predominantly cinnamon but also cloves, nutmeg and other sweet spices.	Use in any food in which cinnamon nutmeg might be used effectively.

1	2	3
4. Barbecue Spice (or Seasoning)	Paprika and such other seasonings as chilli powder, garlic and cloves, with salt and sugar.	Basic seasoning for marinates and basting Sauces. Also in meat casseroles, entre and cheese dishes, dressing.
5. Basil Leaves (or Sweet Basil)	Belongs to mint family; one of the best known herbs. Grown in Europe and U.S.	Famous in tomato dishes; bean, mock turtle and potato soups; good in potato spaghetti, egg dishes, steaks, salad venison, wild duck.
6. Bay Leaves	Dried leaves of edible loured. From Turkey and Portugal.	Famous in pickled beefs, stocks, stews gravis, relishes, spiced vinegar or marinades, in meats, as sauerbraten, etc.
7. Bell Pepper Flakes (or Sweet Pepper)	Dehydrated from sweet green and red peppers.	In salad, sauces, soups, stews, sandwiches fillings. Spanish rice, creoles.
8. Caraway Seed	Dried pungent seeds from herb of the carrot family. Imported from Holland and Poland.	In rye bread, baked goods. Kraut cabbage, potatoes, roast pork, goose cheese, cake, cookies, in Aquavit, Scandinavian liquor.

1	2	3
9. Capers	Low growing shrub of the Mediterranean. Green flower buds and young berries of shrub are pickled.	In fish, chicken, potato, green salads Sauces for fish, lamb, mutton, head cold tongue, and as garnish.
10. Cardamom Seed	Belongs to ginger family. Seeds enclosed in small pod. Seed and pod may be ground together, or only seeds are ground. Put seeds between folds of muslin and pound to powder. Imported from Guatemala and India.	Seeds in pod used in pickling; ground carda mom adds delectable flavour to Danish pastry, coffee cake, fancy rolls Bruised seeds in coffee are delicious.
11. Cassia Bark	From cassia tree. Grown in Malaya. China. Resembles cinnamon flavour. Called Chinese cinnamon.	For pickling, preserving. Ground spice combination with allspice, nutmeg clove. Used in mincemeat.
12. Cassia Buds	Dry unripe fruit of cassia tree.	Pleasing sweet pickling spice.
13. Cayenne (See Red Pepper)		

1	2	3
14. Celery Flakes	Dehydrated from vegetable celery.	In soups, cream sauces, salads, di stuffings, dressing.
15. Celery Seed (also Salt)	Pungent seed from plant botanically different from garden celery. From India.	Croquette mixtures, stews, slew potato salad. Salad dressing, pickles, cheese fish, meat spreads, in stocks and somme.
16. Chervil Leaves	Aromatic herb of carrot family, like parsley but more delicate;	Salads, soups, egg and cheese dishes as a garnish for cold buffet food items
17. Chilli Peppers	A fine satiny surfaced red pepper. Grown in Mexico and Southwest U.S.	Used to make chilli powder for chilly con-carne, tamales pickles, cooking dried beans. Both green and ripe peppers pickled and used to make hot sauces.
18. Chilli Powder	A blend of chilli peppers, cumin seed, oregano, garlic powder, salt, etc.	Most widely used in chilli conclave. Also used in cocktail sauces, gravies stews, appetizers.
19. Chives	Grows indoors or outdoors from small onion-like bulbs. Has mild, onion-like flavour. Also available freeze dried.	Add colour and flavour to cottage and cream cheese, egg and potato dishes soups, salads, disps.

1	2	3
20. Cinnamon	Bark from various trees of the cinnamon family varying in colour from tan to reddish brown.	To flavour pickles, preserves, fruits, hot, drinks and for after-dinner coffee Ground cinnamon used in baked goods puddings, cake, mincemeat.
21. Cinnamon Sugar	Blend of ground cinnamon and sugar.	For sprinkling on buttered toast. Upper crusts of fruit pies, baked apples sugar cookies.
22. Cloves	Nail–shaped dried flower bud of the clove tree. Rich and pungent in flavour. Importrd from Madagascar, Tanzania, Indonesia.	Whole cloves in baked ham. Stocks in pickling and drinks. Ground cloves cakes, cookies, conserves, desserts marinades.
23. Coriander Seed	Bible–time aromatic herb of carrot family. Flavour like lemon peel and sage. Imported from Morocco, Rumania, Argentina.	Spicy seeds used in curry powder, oriental ental candy, pickles, meat product and frank furters.
24. Cumin or "Comino" Seed	Member of carrot family. An Italian and Mexican favourite. Aromatic seeds with bitter warm flavour. Imported from Iran, India, Lebanon.	In chilli powder: cookies, egg and cheese dishes, sauerkraut, soup, meat rice, pickles, sausage, hot tamales.

1	2	3
25. Curry Powder	Blend of spices from India. By varying proportions of 16 spices, different flavoured curries are produced. Contains turmeric, ginger, red pepper, cumin, coriander, etc.	Used to make curries of meat, fish eggs, chicken; curry sauce and flavouring to graves. Adds Oriental touchrice, veal, shrimp, chicken dishes.
26. Dill Weed	Herb of carrot family with aromatic leaves, Seeds and stem. Grows widely in Europe and U.S.	In sauces for potatoes, beans, fish lamb, veal.
27. Dill Seed	Dried tiny fruit of dill plant. Pleasant pungent flavour. From India.	Good in pickles and to garnish split pea and lentil soup.
28. Fennel Seed	From plant of carrot family. Aromatic, resembles arise an dill, but has distinct flavour of its own. From India, Argentina.	Popular with Italians and Scandinavians for rolls, rye bread, other baked goods, bean and lentil soup.
29. File (Gumbo File)	A powder made from dried tender sas-safras leaves. It thickens and flavours.	Used in Creole cookery in place of okra to thicken gumbos.

1	2	3
30. Garlic	Potent favoured bulb of onion family. Flavour either very popular or unpopular. Enjoyable if used with discretion. (Also available as powder, salt, instant minced and chopped.)	Used to enrich flavour of salad dressings, meats, many cooked vegetables, bread, pastas and particularly in dishes from the Mediterranean.
31. Ginger	Dried root of subtropical plant grown in China, Japan, India, British, West Indies, Warm in flavour.	Cracked root used in pickles, preserves, chutney. ground root in cake, ginger-bread, cookies, puddings, soups, pot roasts: Chinese ginger.
32. Horseradish	A large–leaved perennial herb. Grows below the surface of the ground. White-flashed pungent roots. (Also available ground or powdered.)	Grated: used as an appetizer condiment: horseradish sauce: grated and added to cocktail sauce.
33. Italian Seasoning	An herb and red pepper blend which gives Italian characteristic flavour to a wide range of foods.	Used in pizza, spaghetti sauces, salads, cheeses. souffles
34. Juniper Berries	Dried berries of evergreen shrub. With warm pungent flavour.	Used sparingly for spicure's touch in roast venison, lamb, duck, goose, sauerkraut and some stews. Also in ginwhich gives it its flavour.

1	2	3
35. Lemon Pepper	A nippy blend of black pepper and dehydrated lemon.	For broiled meats, poultry and sea-food. Good, too, in tossed green salads.
36. Mace	Lacy covering on inner shell holding nutmeg. Nutmeg tree grows in East and West Indies.	Ground mace good with chocolate. Used in pound and other yellow cake, oyster stew, Spinach. Whole in pickling, preserving and fish sauces.
37. Marjoram Leaves	One of the best known herbs: belongs to mint family. Grown mostly in Europe. Potent in flavour.	Good pounded into veal, used in meat, potato, spinach, cheese, egg and fish dishes: chicken or green vegetable salads. Season poultry stuffings, sausage, stews, soups.
38. Mint (Leaves or Flakes)	A widely grown herb with a delightfully cool, pungent flavour.	Popular in sauce or jelly with roast lamb. Also as edible garnish on carrots, peas, beets.
39. Mixed Pickling Spice	Whole spices usually includes mustard seed, bay leaves, red pepper, cinnamon, allspice ginger.	Used in pickling and preserving meats and to season vegetables, relishes, sauces. Good in stews and soups.

1	2	3
40. Mixed Vegetable Flakes	Includes onion, celery, sweet red and green pepper and carrot flakes.	For use in soups, sauces, stews, casse roles and stuffings. Rehydrate 2/3 as much water and let stand minutes.
41. Mono Sodium Glutamate	Neutral salt of glutamic acid which one of twenty-odd amino acid—the building blocks of all proteins. Is extracted from wheat protein and sugar beets.	Used to heighten flavour in meat, poultry, fish and vegetables dishes.
42. Mustard Seed	Seed of mustard plant grown in England. Europe, Canada and the U.S. Prepared mustard is ground seed blended with other spices and vinegar.	Whole seed in pickles, boiled wit beets, cabbage, sauerkraut. Smart salad garnish. Ground mustard flavours sauce gravies. Prepared mustard in salad dressing, on ham, frankfurters, cheese
43. Nutmeg	Kernel of fruit of the nutmeg tree. Grown in Dutch East Indies and British West Indies. One of the oldest known spices.	Traditional flavouring for baked custard and other desserts. Also used in cream soups, sauces, stews, vegetables suches spinach.

1	2	3
44. Onions (Powder. salt, instant minced, chopped, sliced)	From sweetly pungent varieties of onions.	Power and salt wherever onion flavour is called for. Minced, chopped, et when particles should be visible.
45. Oregano Leaves (or Leaf Oregano)	Is wild marjoram. Has a pleasing, pungent fragrance. From Greece, Mexico, Japan.	Widely used in Mexican and Italian dishes: in meat stews, dried beans, lentils, pizza.
46. Paprika	A red pepper grown in Spain, U. S. and Hungary. Method of grinding determines ultimate flavour. Spanish milder than Hungarian. Rich in Vitamin C.	Used for colour and mild flavour. In fish shell fish, vegetable and egg dishes and in salad dressing.
47. Parsley	Widely grown useful herb. Also available dried.	To season and garnish soups, stews salads, potatoes, stuffing.
48. Pepper, Black and White	Black pepper is dried small, immature berries of climbing vine. White pepper is mature berries with hulls removed. From Indonesia. India and Brazil.	Used whole in pickling, soups, graves and meats. Used ground in most meat vegetables, fish and egg dishes.

1	2	3
49. Pimiento	Ripe fleshy fruit of a sweet pepper plant. Packed in small cans in its own viscous juice.	Used for spots of brilliant colour, mild flavour in soups, stews, salads; as garnish for green vegetables like asparagus green beans.
50. Poppy Seed	Tiny seeds of poppy plant–about 900.000 seeds to the pound. Imported from Holland, Rumania, Turkey, Poland.	Used whole as topping for breads and cookies; as filling for Kolach; in cookies and cake. Garnish for noodles
51. Poultry Seasoning	A mixture of several spices as sage, pepper, marjoram, savoury, thyme, onion powder and celery salt.	Used in poultry, pork, veal and fish stuffings; to season meat loaf, dumplings, biscuit, crusts for meat and poultry pies.
52. Pumpkin Pie Spice	Ground blend of cinnamon, nutmeg, ginger, cloves.	Perfect for pumpkin pie, but use it also for fruit desserts, apple dies and sweet yellow vegetables.
53. Red Pepper	Whole ground or crushed pods of hot red peppers including "Cayenne." From Japan, Africa, Mexico, Turkey, U.S.	Used sparingly to season meats, fish, egg dishes, mayonnaise and other sauces.

1	2	3
54. Rosemary Leaves	Belongs to mint family. Grown in Southern Europe and U.S. Dry, needle–like leaves. Used for flavouring.	Delicious in tomato and egg dishes: soups, fish, Roast lamb, pork, beef and duck, Improves stuffings, vegetable and cheese dishes when combined with sage. In biscuit and muffin mixtures.
55. Saffron	Dried stigmas of a species of purple crocus. Grown in Mediterranean region.	Used pricarily in Spanish and Italian foods for yellow colour as well as flavour in yellow rice, breads, cakes and pea soup.
56. Sage	The most familiar of herbs. Dried leaf of shrub belonging to the mint family. Grown in Yugoslavia and Albania.	Powerful in flavour. Used to season stuffings, sausage, veal and pork dishes, beans, tomatoes and fresh cheese.
57. Savoury Leaves	Grown principally in Southern France. Has a clean balsam fragrance.	Good in boiled fish. Known as the "bean herb." Fine flavour for peas, beans, lentils, fresh or dried: in stuffing, meat balls, croquettes, meat sauces, gravies, egg dishes.

1	2	3
58. Seafood Seasoning	A ground blend of savoury herbs and pungent spices especially handy, when seasoning seafood.	In fish and seafood sauces, chowders, stuffings, breadings.
59. Seasoned Pepper	Black pepper, sweet pepper flakes and other spices.	Convenient seasoning for dozens of meats, poultry, fish salads and sauces.
60. Seasoned Salt	Mixed herbs and spices with salt.	Use as an alternate for part or all of the salt. Added to meat, poultry and egg dishes and in stuffings and sauces.
61. Sesame Seed (or "Benne")	From pods within blossoms of a plant grown in Central America and U.S. Hulled seeds are pearly white with toasted almond flavour.	Baked on rolls, breads and buns to give rich, nutty flavour to crusts. Used in Jewish candy. Halvah. Sesame oil is used in commercial flour mixtures and Chinese stir--fry cooking.
62. Shallots	Small type onion producing large clusters of small bulbs. Also available freeze dried.	Used like garlic to flavour meats, poultry sausage, head cheese, pickles.
63. Shrimp Spice or Crab Boil	Whole spices with emphasis on red peppers, bay leaves, whole peppercorns and mustard.	Addto cooking water for seafood.

1	2	3
64. Sorrel	Belongs to dock family. Long slender leaves used fresh have pleasant acid flavour.	Shredded and added to lettuce, makes lemon juice or vinegar unnecessary. Also in some soups.
65. Soy Sauce	Made from soy beans by a ling curing process.	Used in many Chinese and Japanese dishes.
66. Tabasco*	Made by macerating fresh picked, small hot Mexican peppers, salting and curing 3 years, blending with vinegar, straining, bottling. Produced in Ivory Island.	Used to season egg dishes, gravies, marinades, salad dressings, sauces, sea foods, poultry and soups.
67. Tarragon Leaves	Related to wormwood family. Has aromatic leaves of a slightly bitter flavour. From California, France, Yugoslavia.	Adds excitement to fish, egg and chicken dishes, lobster thermidor, fish sauces, beets, Spinach, aspics. Bernaise Sauce and variations.
68. Thyme Leaves	Grown principally in Spain and Southern France. The No. 2 of American favourite herbs.	An essential in the famous New Orleans cuisine. Present in the French Bouquet Garni. Excellent seasoning for Manhattan Clam

1	2	3
		Chowder, lamb meat soups, stews. Good on vegetables such as carrots, peas, egg plant, escalloped, onions, also in stuffings, stocks and consomme.
69. Turmeric	Root of plant belonging to ginger family. Bright yellow with rich appetizing aroma, and a rather sharp, mustard flavour. From India and Jamaica.	Often combined with mustard for pickling and used in meat and egg dishes. An ingredient of curry powder.

***trade name**

INDEX